GW00630821

MOUNTAIN TROOPS OF THE WAFFEN–SS 1941-1945

Roland Kaltenegger

Translated from the German by Edward Force

Copyright © 1995 by Schiffer Publishing Ltd.
Library of Congress Catalog Number: 94-68641

All rights reserved. No part of this work may be reproduced
or used in any forms or by any means – graphic, electronic
or mechanical, including photocopying or information
storage and retrieval systems – without written permission
from the copyright holder.

This book was originally published under the title
Die Gebirgstruppe der Waffen-SS, 1941-1945
by Podzun Pallas- Verlag.

Printed in the United States of America.
ISBN: 0-88740-813-3

Published by Schiffer Publishing Ltd.
77 Lower Valley Road
Atglen, PA 19310
Please write for a free catalog.
This book may be purchased from the publisher.
Please include $2.95 postage.
Try your bookstore first.

We are interested in hearing from authors with book
ideas on related topics.

Mountain Troops
of the
Waffen–SS

1941–1945

Roland Kaltenegger

Schiffer Military/Aviation History
Atglen, PA

CONTENTS

ACKNOWLEDGEMENTS

In addition to numerous oral and written contributions from former members of Waffen-SS mountain troop divisions and regiments, the following gentlemen and institutions in particular proffered valuable documentation in words and photos. Thus they made sure that this wealth of material would not be thrown away or fall into the wrong hands.

The SS Untersturmführer Felix Benesch, the organizer and first speaker of the Tradition Organization of the 7th SS Volunteer Mountain Division "Prinz Eugen", which conducts an annual gathering along with the 13th Waffen-SS Mountain Division "Handschar" at the Upper Austrian town of Eberschwang in the Innviertel, provided important contact with members of these two mountain organizations.

The SS Hauptsturmführer Joseph Edelbluth of the Tradition Organization of the 6th Mountain Division "Nord" of the former Waffen-SS in the Comradeship of Mountain Troops contacted the entire membership of his mountain-soldier organization.

The SS Hauptsturmführer and Colonel of BGS (retired) Horst Grunwald willingly provided information about his former SS Mountain Jäger Training and Replacement Battalion 13, which was well known as one of the leading support units of the 9th Mountain Division of the German Wehrmacht. The SS Brigade Leader and Major General of the great interest" that the author intended to write about the "Prinz Eugen" and "Handschar" divisions, as he wrote, but also patiently answered many questions.

The SS Obersturmführer Dr. Reinhart Phleps, the always helpful son of the creator and first commander of the 7th SS Volunteer Mountain Division "Prinz Eugen" and the first commanding general of the V. SS Mountain Corps, made numerous important documentations and photographs available to the author, as well as allowing many a look into the multiple volumes of the war diaries of his father Artur Phleps.

The SS Sturmbannführer Albert Stenwedel of the 13th Waffen-SS Mountain Division "Handschar", who also performed particular services for the organization of Knight's Cross bearers, was not only a critical advisor to the author, but on the basis of his many functions, was able to make contact with numerous mountain soldiers of the Waffen-SS and make several interesting documents available.

Of the holders of the Knight's Cross among the mountain troops of the Waffen-SS, there were not only Otto Kumm, holder of the oak leaves and swords of the Knight's Cross of the Iron Cross, and Albert Stenwedel, holder of the Knight's Cross, but, among others, also SS Hauptsturmführer Franz Josef Krombholz.

Thanks are also due to the Berlin Document Center, the Federal Archives in Koblenz, the Federal Military Archives at Freiburg in the Breisgau, the Institute for History of the Times in Munich, the Munin publishing house and the Tradition Organization of the 6th Waffen-SS Mountain Division "Nord", in the Comradeship of the Mountain Troops.

Roland Kaltenegger
Munich-Kolbermoor, Upper Bavaria
Autumn 1994

Training in the mountains.

I. The Mountain Troops of the Waffen-SS

Himmler's ambition had not yet been satisfied. After he had succeeded, as a result of the Röhm Putsch, in turning the Third Reich from a storm-trooper to a secret-police state, he had the desire to become known as a field marshal too. With the change from the Storm Department (SA) to the Security Police (SS), the first step was made. The second took place with the change of the SS Verfügungstruppe (SS-VT) into the Waffen-SS. But the Reichsführer was still not satisfied with that. For during the years of peace and war from 1935 to 1945, the Wehrmacht had succeeded, despite many difficulties, in establishing a powerful mountain troop of, in the end, eleven mountain divisions, nine higher command offices, and additional mountain-related troops — which were finally united into the four high-mountain Jäger battalions and the ski Jäger regiments — and to deploy those troops on all European fronts from the Arctic to Monte Cassino and from the Western Alps to the Caucasus.[1]

The longer World War II lasted, and the more successfully the mountain divisions of the Wehrmacht operated on the battlefields in Poland and France, Scandinavia and the Balkans, the more Heinrich Himmler was determined to have his own mountain troops in the ranks of the Waffen-SS. As a result, appropriate mountain units were established in the course of the years. From the beginning, the SS Reichsführer took part in their development. Thus there originated, among others, one SS mountain division, one SS volunteer mountain division, three Waffen-SS mountain divisions, one Waffen-SS mountain (Karstjäger) division, the Waffen-SS mountain brigades and regiments, a General Command of the SS Mountain Corps and Corps Troops, a General Command of the Waffen Mountain Army Corps and Corps Troops, as well as the High Mountain School of the Waffen-SS in Neustift, located in the Stubai Valley of Tirol.

For these purposes, Himmler not only gave the appropriate commands and orders, and equipped his mountain units with the right uniforms and equipment for their various tasks, but also honored these elite troops with a special edelweiss emblem, which could be worn on the mountain caps and uniforms of all ranks of mountain soldiers in the Waffen-SS.

Sleeve and cap insignia of the Waffen-SS mountain troops.

Now the mountain troops of the Wehrmacht were no longer alone in combat in Scandinavia, in the Balkans, and in Germany at the Semmering Pass and on the upper Rhine, but were supported effectively in these theaters of war by two command offices and six mountain divisions of the Waffen-SS. And in addition, the cooperation between the mountain troops of the Wehrmacht and those of the Waffen-SS was sometimes so close that, in addition to the usual conditions of who was subordinate to whom, there were actual mergers of individual units. Thus in the last weeks of World War II, the 9th Mountain Division of the Wehrmacht existed as the "Battle Group Semmering" or "Battle Group Raithel" and consisted of training and replacement units. Men of the Mountain Jäger Junior Leader School, the Mountain Artillery School, the SS Mountain Jäger Training and Replacement Battalion 13, all the flying personnel of Battle Squadron "Boelke", emergency units, members of the Navy, and Styrian Volkssturm men united into a highly effective combat unit.[2]

This crudely formed large unit made up of members of the Luftwaffe, Navy, Wehrmacht and Waffen-SS protected the approaches to Styria in a broad sector, including Semmering and Hochwechsel, from the massive attacks of the Red Army, sometimes being closely linked with the 1st People's Mountain Division. Thanks to these two mountain divisions, the troops of the German Sixth Army could be withdrawn to the west successfully in some semblance of order.[3] On the basis of this unique cooperation, a special attitude of loyalty developed between the mountain troops of the Wehrmacht and the Waffen-SS, characterized by mutual respect and recognition that have endured to this day. It was not without reason that, for example, not only the 9th Mountain Division, with its mixture of Wehrmacht and Waffen-SS soldiers, but also the Tradition Organization of the 6th SS Mountain Division "Nord" became members of the Comradeship of Mountain Troops in the fifties.

While the volunteers and Waffen-SS mountain divisions saw service from 1942 to 1945 exclusively in the Balkans, the eternal crisis area of Europe, with its centuries-old nationality conflicts between the Roman Catholic Croats, the Serbian Orthodox Serbs and the Mohammedan Bosniaks (to mention only a few ethnic trouble sources),[4] the 6th SS Mountain Division "Nord" fought from 1941 to 1945 in the Scandinavian Theater of War at the place where the 20th Mountain Army of Generaloberst Dietl joined the Finnish army of Marshal von Mannerheim. According to the military situations of the times, it was even subordinated to the Third Finnish Army Corps for a time, but also fought shoulder to shoulder with its Edelweiss comrades of the Wehrmacht mountain troops. Indeed, the connections and relations between the 6th SS Mountain Division "Nord" and the 7th Mountain Division of the Wehrmacht, as well as the "Kräutler" Division Group, were so close that at times units of the Wehrmacht mountain divisions were even subordinated to the SS mountain troops, and in certain operations troop units of the Waffen-SS mountain forces were subordinated to the Army's mountain troops.[5]

All in all, the units of the Waffen-SS were only seldom stronger, in terms of equipment and manpower, than the comparable units of the Wehrmacht. There were two reasons for this: First, the Waffen-SS consisted at first almost exclusively of volunteers; second, its function as "front-line firemen" demanded better organization and equipment, though in many cases this was not available to the mountain troops of the Waffen-SS. Still in all, the mountain troops of the Waffen-SS mountain divisions, unlike the mountain divisions of the Wehrmacht, had the advantage of an SS flak unit. The 6th SS Mountain Division "Nord", in fact, was composed of four infantry or mountain Jäger regiments.

II. The Command Offices of the SS Mountain Troops

They corresponded to those of the Wehrmacht. Of the eighteen general commands of the Waffen-SS, two pertained to the mountain troops. They were the General Command of the V. SS Mountain Corps and the General Command of the IX. Waffen-SS Mountain Army Corps, which saw action exclusively in the Balkans.[6]

1. The General Command, V. SS Mountain Corps

a) Origin

The establishment of the corps was carried out by the SS-FHA on July 1, 1943, with the establishment directive of July 8, 1943, and with the corps staff in Berlin and the corps troops at the Milowitz Troop Training Camp near Prague. In the summer of the same year, it was assembled in Yugoslavia, and it fought against partisans in the Balkans, in Bosnia-Mostar. Before it capitulated in the Berlin area in May 1945, it saw service around Frankfurt on the Oder from February to April 1945, and was renamed:

V. SS Volunteer Mountain Army Corps
V. SS Mountain Corps
V. SS Volunteer Mountain Corps.

b) Structure

Corps Intelligence Unit, General Command V, SS Mountain Corps / SS Mountain Corps Intelligence Unit 105 / 505

SS Reconnaissance Unit 105 / 505 (Motorcycle rifle battalion)
SS Panzer Unit, General Command, V. SS Mountain Corps / SS Panzer Unit 105 / 505
SS Panzer Company 105
SS Assault Gun Unit 105
SS Artillery Unit 105 / SS Heavy Artillery Unit 505
SS Flak Unit 105 (ex-SS Heavy Flak Unit 7)
SS Launcher Unit 105 / SS Launcher Unit 500
SS Launcher Battery 521
SS Medical Unit 105 / SS Medical Company (mot) 505
SS Supply Troop 105 / SS Supply Company (mot) 105
SS Assault Battalion, V. SS Mountain Corps (as of April 1945)
SS Assault Gun Unit "Skanderbeg" (as of April 1945)
SS Flight Echelon
SS Corps Map Office (mot) 105
SS Heavy Observation Battery (mot)
SS Defensive Geological Battalion 105
SS Motorcycle Rifle Battalion, V. SS Mountain Corps
SS Horsedrawn Transport Column 105
SS Corps Supply Leader
SS Supply Regiment (mot) 105
SS Motorcycle Company 105
SS Vehicle Repair Company 105 (1st & 2nd)
SS Clothing Repair Company (mot) 105
SS Veterinary Examination Office 105
SS Corps Horse Hospital 105
SS Field Post Office (mot) 105
SS Corps Security Company 105
Driving School, General Command, V. SS Mountain Corps

SS Karstwehr Battalion
SS Panzer Unit 7
Plus all the staff and corps troops, numbered 105.

c) Commanding Generals

SS Obergruppenführer and General of the Waffen-SS
Artur Phleps 4/21/1943 — 9/21/1944
SS Obergruppenführer and General of the Waffen-SS
Friedrich-Wilhelm Krüger February 1945 — March 1945
SS Obergruppenführer and General of the Waffen-SS and Police
Friedrich Jeckeln March 1945 — May 1945

2. The General Command, IX. Waffen-SS Mountain Corps

a) Origin

The establishment of the corps was carried out on May 29, 1944, and was completed in July in Croatia to command the Albanian and Croatian units of the Waffen-SS. During the partisan fighting in the Balkans, the two Croatian Waffen-SS mountain divisions, the "Handschar" and "Kama", were subordinated to it. Later, during the fighting in Hungary in 1944-1945 (in the Budapest region in 1945), the 8th SS Cavalry Division "Florian Geyer" and the 22nd SS Volunteer Cavalry Division "Maria Theresia" were subordinated to the Corps. On February 12, 1945 the Corps was annihilated in Budapest.

b) Structure
SS Corps Map Office (mot)
SS Tank Destroyer Unit 509
SS Mountain Artillery Regiment 509
SS Flak Unit 509
SS Reconnaissance Unit 509
SS Mountain Engineer Battalion 509
SS Motor Vehicle Company
SS Motor Vehicle Repair Platoon
SS Field Hospital 509
SS Motor Vehicle Platoon 509
SS Field Post Office (mot)
SS Field Police Troop (mot)
SS Corps Security Company (mot)
SS Intelligence Unit (mot) 109
SS Supply Troop 109
Plus all staff and corps troops with the number 109.

c) Commanding Generals

SS Obergruppenführer and General of the Waffen-SS
Karl-Gustav Sauberzweig Summer 1944 — December 1944
SS Obergruppenführer and General of the Police
Karl Pfeffer von Wildenbruch December 1944 — 2/12/1945

III. The Mountain Divisions of the Waffen-SS

During World War II no fewer than 38 Waffen-SS divisions were established. Six of them belonged to the SS mountain troops — these being the 6th SS Mountain Division "Nord", the 7th SS Volunteer Mountain Division "Prinz Eugen", the 13th Waffen-SS Mountain Division "Handschar" (Croatian No. 1), the 21st Waffen-SS Mountain Division "Skanderbeg" (Albanian No. 1), the 23rd Waffen-SS Mountain Division "Kama" (Croatian No. 2), and the 24th Waffen-SS Mountain Division "Karstjäger."[7]

1. The 6th SS Mountain Division "Nord"

a) Origin
The SS Mountain Division "Nord" was first established in Norway as the SS Battle Group "Nord" from the staff of the Commander of the Waffen-SS in Norway. As of September 1941 it existed as the SS Division "Nord" with:
SS Infantry Regiment 6 (mot) I-III (ex-SS Totenkopf-Standarte 6 in Prague)
SS Infantry Regiment 7 (mot) I-III (ex-SS Totenkopf-Standarte 7 in Brno)
SS Infantry Regiment 9 (mot) I-III (ex-SS Totenkopf-Standarte Kirkenes)
Reconnaissance Unit, SS Battle Group/Division "Nord"
Artillery Regiment, SS Battle Group/Division "Nord", I-III
Flak Unit, SS Battle Group/Division "Nord"
Engineer Battalion, SS Battle Group/Division "Nord"
Intelligence Unit, SS Battle Group/Division "Nord"
Division Supply Leader, SS Battle Group/Division "Nord"
Supply units of SS Battle Group/Division "Nord"[8]

The reconstruction into a mountain division in Ticino had been ordered on January 15, 1942, and changed on March 3, 1942. Since only two mountain Jäger battalions, one rifle battalion and one unit each of light and heavy artillery could be formed out of the two SS Infantry Regiments 6 and 7, the formation of the lacking troop units was carried out at the Wildflecken training camp in Germany. There, in the Rhoen area, in addition to the SS Assault Brigades "Wallonien"[9] and "Charlemagne" (Karl der Grosse), the Mountain Jäger Battalions I to IV and two mountain artillery units were formed new for the 6th SS Mountain Division "Nord" and transferred to Finland during the course of the summer.[10]

b) Division Names
SS Battle Group "Nord": 2/28/1941 — September 1941
SS Division "Nord": September 1941 — 5/15/1942
SS Mountain Division "Nord": 5/15/1942 — 10/22/1943
6th SS Mountain Division "Nord": 10/22/1943 — May 1945

Bergführer emblem of the Waffen-SS mountain troops.

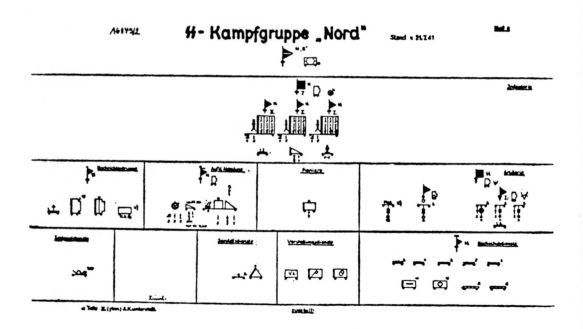

Tactical structure of the Battle Group as of 7/21/1941.

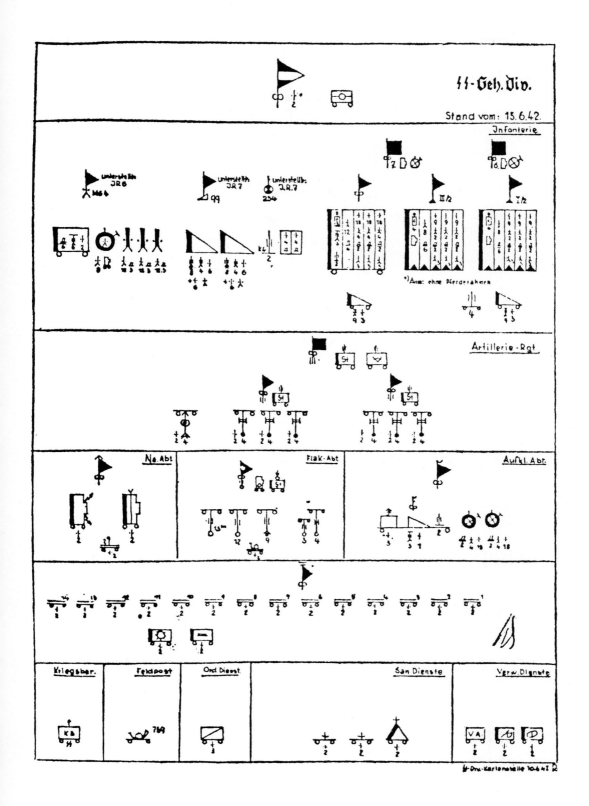

Tactical structure of the Division as of 6/15/1942.

13

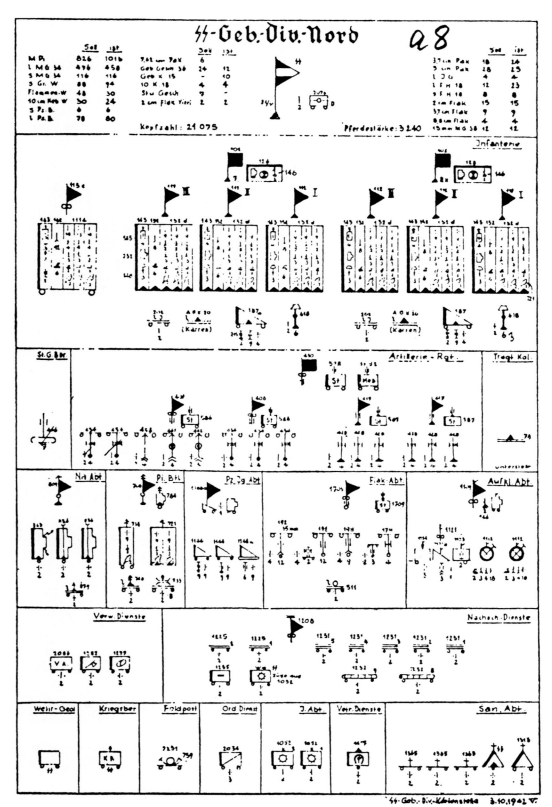

Tactical structure of the Division as of 10/2/1942.

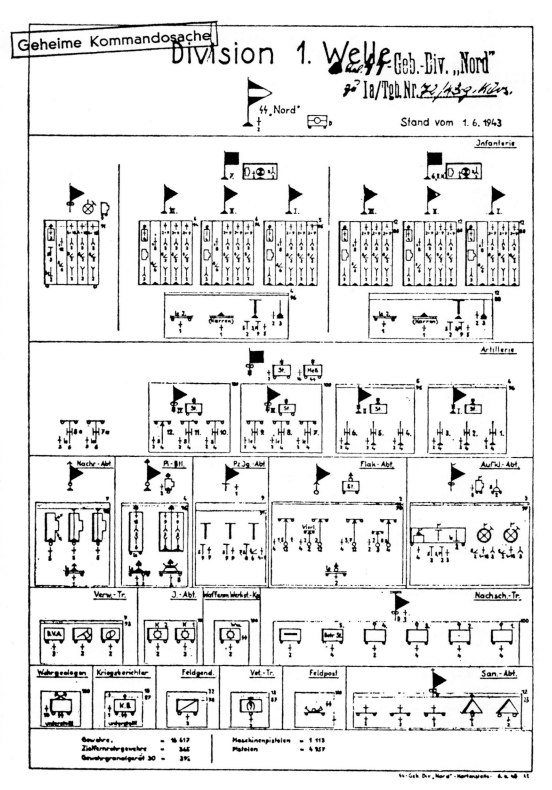

Geheime Kommandosache

Tactical structure of the Division as of 6/1/1943.

c) Structure

SS Mountain Jäger Regiment 11 "Reinhard Heydrich"
SS Mountain Jäger Regiment 12 "Michael Gaissmair"
SS Mountain Artillery Regiment 6
SS Infantry Regiment (mot) 5
SS Infantry Regiment 9
SS Panzer Grenadier Battalion 506
SS Rifle Battalion "Nord" (mot)
SS (Mountain) Panzerjäger Unit 6
SS Assault Gun Battery 6
SS Flak Unit 6
SS Mountain Intelligence Unit 6
SS Mountain Reconnaissance Unit (mot) 6
SS Mountain Engineer Battalion 6
SS Ski(jäger) Battalion "Norge"
SS Repair Unit 6
SS Clothing Company 6
SS Mountain Medical Unit 6
SS Veterinary Company 6
SS Mountain Intelligence Platoon 6
SS Field Police Troop 6
SS-og Political Company (Norwegian unit)
SS Storekeeping Battalion 6
SS Administrative Troop Unit 6
SS Canine Echelon 6
SS Field Replacement Battalion 6
SS Launcher Unit 6

(Division troops — such as the Commander of SS Supply Troops No. 6 — with the SS number 6)

d) War Service

From April to June 1941 it guarded the coasts of southern and northern Norway (Kirkenes-Vardö). Then it prepared to attack the USSR in Finland west of Salla and on the Liza. In the fighting for the fortifications around Salla, the mountain soldiers of the Waffen-SS faced their first and worst crisis, briefly putting their further action in question. But then, in the fighting for the Kuolajärvi sector, the encirclement action near Nurmi and the pursuit to the Voyta sector, they proved themselves well. The fight to encircle the fortified Lyssaya area and Voyta sector, the combat around the Sohyana sector and Kiestinki, the defensive battles east of Kiestinki, the fighting on both sides of the Kangaswaara and the combat around the Liza during the third offensive on Dietl's fateful river, and the extension of the bridgehead east of the Liza turned out to be just as difficult as the defensive action on the Liza and the defense of northern Finland.[11]

The war year of 1942 proceeded as follows for the 6th SS Mountain Division "Nord": Defensive fighting in northern Finland, defensive fighting near Kiestinki, action within the framework of the III. Finnish Army Corps in the Salla-Kairala-Alakurtti area, later in the command area of the XVIII. Mountain Army Corps, in the Kananainen-Sohyana-Kiestinki area, then an advance toward Louchi on both sides of the "Road of the SS" and northward in the direction of Okunyeva-Guba-Tiek Lake as well as along the "Road of the Mountain Jäger" and to the northeast in the direction of Nyatovara.[12]

The war year of 1943 was characterized by the positional warfare in Karelia and participation in the fighting for the rear bunkers, fought out shoulder to shoulder, in an extremely close condition of command and subordination between the 7th Mountain Division and parts of the 6th SS Mountain Division "Nord."[13]

tain Army Corps in northern Finland, in the war zone of Sohyana-Kiestinki-Kuusamo-Hyrynsalmi-Oulu-Pudasjärvi-Kemi-Tornio-Rovaniemi-Munio with the Division Group "Kräutler", the later 10th Mountain Division and the 7th Mountain Division. Later the withdrawal took place, at first within the XXXVI. Mountain Army Corps in the Kairala-Salla combat area, and then within the Corps-Group Rübel in the Kolosyoki Road-Arctic Road combat area to relieve and protect the flanks of the 2nd Mountain Division. At the beginning of 1945 came the retreat across the Sturmbock position to the Lyngen Fjord and from there via Skibotn, Narvik and Fauske to the Mo area. From here they were transported by ship and rail to the Oslo area for transfer to Denmark.

The war year of 1945 began for the 6th SS Mountain Division "Nord" with their transfer to the Western Front. In March they took part in a last offensive from the Landau-Pirmasens area toward Lorraine. Then they took a defensive position on the Bitsch-Zinsweiler-Niederbronn line. There followed the defensive combat in the Saarland and on the Ruwer as well as in the Trier area, the retreat over the Hunsrück Highroad to the north. In the framework of the 2nd Mountain Division, the mountain soldiers of the Waffen-SS fought shoulder to shoulder with those of the Wehrmacht on their withdrawal to the Worms area. Between March and May there was combat action in the bridgehead at Boppard, the withdrawal across the Rhine and farther to the northeast into the Hessian area. Parts of the division reached Thuringia and Bavaria, where they finally capitulated and were taken prisoner by the Americans. [14]

e) Division Commanders

SS Brigade Führer and Generalmajor of the Waffen-SS
Richard Herrmann 6/12/1940-5/25/1941
SS Gruppenführer and Generalleutnant of the Waffen-SS
Karl Demelhuber 5/25/1941-4/20/1942
SS Brigade Führer and Generalmajor of the Waffen-SS
Matthias Kleinheisterkamp 4/1/1942-12/15/1943
SS Gruppenführer and Generalleutnant of the Waffen-SS
Lothar Debes 12/15/1943-May 1944
SS Obergruppenführer and General of the Waffen-SS
Friedrich-Wilhelm Krüger May 1944-8/23/1944
SS Standartenführer
Gustav Lombard (m.d.F.b.) 8/23/1944-9/1/1944
SS Gruppenführer und Generalleutnant of the Waffen-SS
Karl Heinrich Brenner 9/1/1944-May 1945

f) Insignia

The members of the 6th SS Mountain Division "Nord" wore shoulder patches with the lettering "Nord." Members of SS Mountain Jäger Regiment 11 "Reinhard Heydrich" bore the inscription "Reinhard Heydrich" on their shoulder patches. The members of SS Mountain Jäger Regiment 12 "Michael Gaissmair" had the lettering "Michael Gaissmair" on their shoulder patches. The members of SS Ski(jäger) Battalion (Norwegian) wore shoulder patches with the inscription "Norge", and the SS-og Political Company wore shoulder patches with the lettering "Frw. Legion Norwegen" (Norwegian Volunteer Legion).

g) Division Emblem

The members of the 6th SS Mountain Division "Nord" wore, instead of the death's-head, the runic symbol of the Waffen-SS on the right lapel of their uniform. The Hagal Rune — a life-and-death rune —was used on vehicles as their tactical symbol.

Cuff Title and (below) division emblem of the 6th SS Mountain Division "Nord."

Cuff Title and (below) division emblem of the 7th SS Volunteer Mountain Division "Prinz Eugen."

2. The 7th SS Volunteer Mountain Division "Prinz Eugen"

a) Structure

The division was being formed since the spring of 1942. It was formed by drafting 15,000 ethnic Germans in the Serbian Banat, where the ethnic Germans numbered only 130,000, but also in Siebenbürgen in Batschka, Syrmia and Slavonia, in order to replace the heavy Waffen-SS losses in the Balkans.

In the summer of 1942 it was structured as follows:
SS Mountain Jäger Regiment 1, Battalions I to IV
SS Mountain Jäger Regiment 2, Battalions I to IV
SS Cycle Battalion
SS Cavalry Unit
SS Panzer Unit
SS Mountain Artillery Regiment, Units I to IV
SS Engineer Battalion
SS Intelligence Unit
SS Mountain Jäger Replacement Battalion
Supply Troops
In the winter of 1942-1943 the following units were added:
SS Reconnaissance Unit
SS Panzerjäger Unit
SS Motorcycle Rifle Battalion
SS Flak Unit
In the summer of 1943, the motorcycle rifle battalion was disbanded and the SS Mountain Jäger Regiment 1 was strengthened by two companies. In addition, a field replacement battalion of five companies was formed. On October 22, 1943, in the course of renaming the Waffen-SS units, the division was renamed the 7th SS Volunteer Mountain Division "Prinz Eugen." The two mountain Jäger regiments were now called SS Volunteer Mountain Jäger Regiment 13 "Artur Phleps" and SS Volunteer Mountain Jäger Regiment 14 "Skanderbeg." The other units were given the number 7. After the heavy losses at Nisch in October 1944, the division was renewed again, without being given new field post numbers. It was captured by the Yugoslavians at Cilli in 1945.[15]

b) Division Names

SS Division "Prinz Eugen" March 1942
SS Volunteer Division "Prinz Eugen" 4/1/1942-1943
SS Volunteer Mountain Division "Prinz Eugen" 1943-10/22/1943
7th SS Volunteer Mountain Division "Prinz Eugen" 10/22/1943-May 1945

c) Structure

SS Volunteer Mountain Jäger Regiment 13 "Artur Phleps"
SS Volunteer Mountain Jäger Regiment 14 "Skanderbeg"
SS Volunteer Mountain Artillery Regiment 7
SS Panzer Unit 7
(light) SS Panzer Company
SS Mountain Panzerjäger Unit 7
SS Cavalry Unit 7
SS Assault Gun Unit/Battery 7
SS Flak Unit 7 (later transferred to V. SS Mountain Corps)
SS Flak Company
SS Mountain Intelligence Unit 7
SS Volunteer Mountain Reconnaissance Unit (mot) 7

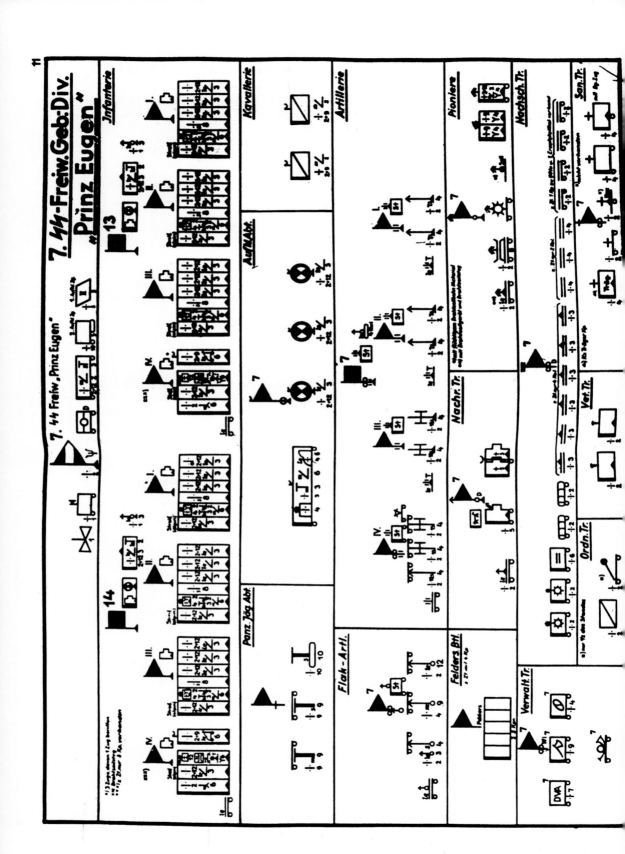

SS Panzer Reconnaissance Platoon   SS Volunteer Mountain Veterinary Company 1/7, 2/7
SS Cycle Battalion   SS Volunteer Mountain Intelligence Platoon 7
SS Cycle Reconnaissance Unit 7   SS Propaganda Platoon
SS Mountain Engineer Battalion 7   SS Field Police Troop 7
SS Motorcycle Rifle Battalion 7   SS Field Replacement Battalion 7
SS Supply Company 7   SS Repair Unit 7
SS Repair Shop Company/Platoon   SS Geological Battalion
SS Storekeeping Battalion 7
SS Medical Unit 7
(Division troops — such as the Commander, SS Supply Troops 7 — with SS number 7)

d) War Service

Between 1942 and 1943, the 7th Volunteer Mountain Division "Prinz Eugen" saw service exclusively in the Balkans — more precisely: After its formation, it was summoned to the Uzice-Pozega-Cacak Slatina-Kraljevo area in October 1942 to fight against partisans and secure toe occupied regions. In December it was transferred to the Karlovac area southwest of Agram and took part in Operation "Weiss" there. Then came the battles at Planina, Bes.-Petrovac and Lapac Grn in the Bihac area, followed by the advance from the Livno area toward Mostar and then the combat at Kupres, Tonislavgrad, Lipe, Posuje and in the Siroki Brijec-Glamock area. Then came the securing of the important bauxite mines in the Ljubinski area and the supply route from Sarajevo to Mostar.

As of April 1943, the "Prinz Eugen" Division saw service in western Montenegro, at first in carrying out Operation "Schwarz", in which it saw action fighting against partisan bands in the Stolag-Blagaj-Podgorica-Lisino Gora-Slavnik areas as well as in the Piva sector. Then came securing tasks in the Sarajevo-Viosko area, in the Tuzla region as far as Bosnia at Bistrica, and in the area of Mostar to secure the bauxite mining area. At the beginning of September 1943 the disarmament of the Italians after Mussolini's fall and the switch of the former Axis partner to the Allied side took place in the Metkovic-Dubci area after a march to the coast. Then came an advance on Split and combat in the Split area and on the Peljesac Peninsula in the region of the mouth of the Neretva, as well as the occupation of the islands of Brac, Hvar and Korcula. At the end of November the Division was relieved of securing the coast and prepared for Operation "Kugelblitz" eastward of Sarajevo. There followed battles against Tito's partisans in the Rogatica-Gorazde-Sokolac area, and then pursuit fighting in the Zenica and Bogojno-Livno areas. The large-scale and very successful Operation "Kugelblitz", in which once again there was combat action shared by the mountain troops of the Waffen-SS and the Wehrmacht, is mentioned as follows in the "War Diary of the High Command of the Wehrmacht":

December 7, 1943: "In the Operation "Kugelblitz", the 1st Mountain Division gained further success. The partisan bands retreated to the north before the SS Mountain Division "Prinz Eugen." The Eleusis and Kalamata airfields were attacked by strong enemy air forces, with four of our places destroyed and 17 damaged." [16]

December 20, 1943: "The enemy losses in Operation "Kugelblitz" amounted to some 9000 men in all. 24 guns, 6 armored vehicles and numerous infantry weapons were captured. Thus despite the roughest terrain and weather conditions, we were generally successful in smashing the communist forces in eastern Bosnia and thwart the enemy's operative intention to advance into the old Serbian area. In order to attack the enemy, who had broken through the enclosing ring in a northwesterly direction, in immediate pursuit and wipe them out, the V. SS Mountain Army Corps again entered a broad front with the mass of its units that took part in Operation "Kugelblitz" and moved to the northwest and west." [17]

Between January and September 1944 the "Prinz Eugen" was sent to fight against partisan bands, at first in the Travnik-Kupres-Livno areas during Operation "Waldrausch", then at Kalinovik, Rogatica and Vakuf, and then during Operation "Maibaum" south and southeast of Olovo. During "Rösselsprung" at the end of May 1944, it took part in a large-scale operation against Tito's partisan bands, but despite all its efforts, it did not succeed in immobilizing and capturing the Yugoslav partisan leader and his staff. Then came the pursuit fighting in the Vranina Planina and in the Brod-Maglaj-Vrbas-Teslic area. At the end of September it was transferred to the region of Nisch and then saw action north and south of that city, against Soviet and Bulgarian forces. Now the wartime events in the Balkans came fast and furious for the 7th SS Volunteer Mountain Division "Prinz Eugen": Combat at Zajecar and Leskovac — Gradelica came on each other's heels, along with the retreat fighting on the Morava on both sides of Nisch, then again through Krusevac into the Kraljevo area; the defensive fighting on both sides of the bridgehead of Kraljevo, which was particularly strenuous but successful in the end; the withdrawal combat through Adrani, Cacak, Rogatica, Ljuboviba and Zvornik into the Janja region; the freeing of the withdrawal route at Janja-Bijeljina and the settling at the bridgehead on the Save; the defensive fighting at the Brcko bridgehead as well as between the Danube and the Bosu on both sides of Sid. [18]

It was the beginning of 1945 when the "Prinz Eugen" Division saw action in the Papuk Mountains. Attacks in the Vocin-Podrav Slatina area and on the southern edge of the mountains near Slavonska Pozega were the result. But then came action in the region of Sarajevo, and especially the freeing of the approach to Sarajevo near Trnovo. The operations carried out there were called "Frühlingssturm" (Spring Storm), "Wehrwolf" (Werewolf) and "Frühlingserwachen" (Spring's Awakening). In April the withdrawal fighting from the Sarajevo area began, moving through Zenica and Doboj across the Save in the Dubocac region and near Slavonski Brod. In the "War Diary of the High Command of the Wehrmacht" one can read, among other things:

Situation Book 3/31/1945: "The fighting at Sarajevo decreased. The road to Zenica is barred by partisan bands and is now supposed to be opened by a regiment of the 7th SS Mountain Division. Operation "Maigewitter" (May Storm) was broken off near Tuzla." [19]

Now the division moved on through Nova Gradiska and Banova Jaruga into the region of Agram. The "Prinz Eugen" Division was removed from the withdrawal movement at the end of the month and transferred to the Karlovac region, southwest of Agram. In the Daruvar area it was then turned off and sent in the direction of Laibach, so that it was spared action in the "Adriatic Coastland" zone of operations under General of the Mountain Troops Ludwig Kübler, centered around Fiume. After the withdrawal fighting, the exhausted troop units moved through Sambor into the Cilli region, where they fell into merciless Yugoslavian imprisonment. [20]

e) Division Commanders
SS Gruppenführer and Generalleutnant of the Waffen-SS
Artur Phleps 3/1/1942-6/21/1943
SS Brigadeführer and Generalmajor of the Waffen-SS
Karl Reichsritter von Oberkamp 7/3/1943-2/1/1944
SS Brigadeführer and Generalmajor of the Waffen-SS
Otto Kumm 8/1/1944-1/20/1945
SS Brigadeführer and Generalmajor of the Waffen-SS
August Schmidhuber 1/20/1945-May 1945

f) Insignia
The members of the 7th SS Volunteer Mountain Division "Prinz Eugen" wore shoulder patches with the inscription "Prinz Eugen." Members of the SS Volunteer Mountain Jäger Regiment 13 "Artur Phleps" wore shoulder patches with the name "Artur Phleps." The members of the SS Volunteer Mountain Jäger Regiment 14 "Skanderbeg" had the name "Skanderbeg" on their shoulder patches.

g) Division Emblem
The Odal Rune, which was worn instead of the SS Sigrune on the right collar patch and also used as a tactical symbol on the motor vehicles, had the form of a diamond with X-patterned legs.

SS Obergruppenführer and General of the Waffen-SS Artur Phleps, former officer of the Imperial and Royal Army, after 1918 a high officer in the Romanian Army, in World War II the first commander of the 7th SS Volunteer Mountain Division "Prinz Eugen" and finally commander of the V. SS Mountain Corps.

3. The 13th Waffen-SS Mountain Division "Handschar"

a) Origin

The 13th Waffen-SS Mountain Division "Handschar" (Croatian No. 1) was established in Bosnia and Herzegovina on March 1, 1943, on the basis of the Führer's order of February 10, 1943, as the Croatian SS Volunteer Division, made up of Croatian volunteers, all of whom were Moslems. "The Moslem Bosniaks had taken a rather negative attitude to the Croatian state, and the Poglavnik would have preferred setting up a Croatian Ustascha Division through the SS instead. When recruiting began, the Croatian government caused difficulties and drafted the volunteers into the Croatian Army or shut them away in Croatian concentration camps, which Himmler soon had searched. The establishment order was given on April 30, 1943." [21]

The establishment of the division staff took place in Agram, while the intelligence unit was set up in Goslar, and the division as a whole was assembled in the backlands of the military zone in southern France, with the division staff quartered in Le Puy, later Le Rozier. According to Tessin, it consisted of the following units:

Croatian SS Volunteer Mountain Jäger Regiment 1
Croatian SS Volunteer Mountain Jäger Regiment 2
Croatian SS Volunteer Mountain Artillery Regiment (Div. 13)
Croatian SS Cavalry Unit (Div. 13)
Croatian SS Reconnaissance Unit (Div. 13)
Croatian SS Panzerjäger Unit (Div. 13)
Croatian SS Flak Unit (Div. 13)
Croatian SS Engineer Battalion (Div. 13)
Croatian SS Intelligence Unit (Div. 13)
SS supply troops (Div. 13)

The "War Diary of the High Command of the Wehrmacht" tells the following about this large mountain unit of the Waffen-SS:

"An important strengthening of the OB Southeast was provided by the 13th SS (Bosniak) Mountain Division, which was transported from the Neuhammer Troop Training Camp to Slavonic-Brod in the middle of February 1944. On February 13 the ideas which the Reichsführer-SS had in mind when he formed this division were communicated. It was pointed out that — if the division was to fulfill the hopes placed in it — much attention should be given to the ethnic characteristics of the Moslem Bosniaks, whom the German command personnel had been trained to control strictly. Of special significance to the division was the Great Mufti (the one in Jerusalem, Mohammed Emin el-Huseini). The transfer of the division to Croatia should fulfill the promise of the Reich to return to the population their drafted sons again, and a wave of general confidence should be inspired among the people. The division should first be assembled in Syrmia; its first task should be the subduing of the area between Drina and Bosna; only after that should active participation in the fighting against partisan bands be considered." [22]

But that was not all. According to an order of September 26, 1944, the Moslems in the 23rd Waffen-SS Mountain Division "Kama", then in southern Hungary, should be transferred to the "Handschar"only for the two Waffen-SS Mountain Jäger Regiments 27 and 28, each gaining two battalions, one engineer company, one intelligence company and one field replacement battalion. The reconnaissance unit, the Panzerjäger unit, the mountain artillery regiment and the mountain engineer battalion were declared, according to Tessin, to be special troops of the Reichsführer-SS and were given the number 509. "To the 6015 German officers, junior officers and men there should be additions from Army 3000, which was previously active in Crete. With the evacuation of Croatia, Croatian nationals should be discharged." [23]

With that, the 13th Waffen-SS Mountain Division "Handschar" (Croatian No. 1) had ceased to exist. "In its place," according to Stein, "there remained the abbreviated and predominantly German 13th SS Mountain Regimental Group "Handschar", and this unit, not the "brave Moslems", fought later on the Drau front." [24] There the remaining men were taken prisoner by the British.

b) Division Names

Croatian SS Volunteer Division 3/1/1943-7/2/1943
Croatian SS Volunteer Mountain Division 7/2/1943-10/9/1943
SS Volunteer Mountain Division (Croatian) 10/9/1943-10/22/1943
13th SS Volunteer Mountain Division (Croatian) 10/22/1943-June 1944
13th Waffen-SS Mountain Division "Handschar" (Croatian No. 1) June 1944-end

c) Structure

Waffen-SS Mountain Jäger Regiment 27
Waffen-SS Mountain Jäger Regiment 28
Croatian SS Volunteer Mountain Artillery Regiment / SS Volunteer Mountain Artillery Regiment 13 / SS Mountain Artillery Regiment 13 / Waffen-SS Artillery Regiment 13
Croatian SS Panzer Unit
Croatian SS Panzerjäger Unit / SS Mountain Panzerjäger Unit 13
Croatian SS Cavalry Unit
Croatian SS Flak Unit / SS Flak Unit 13
Croatian SS Intelligence Unit / SS Mountain Intelligence Unit 13
SS Reconnaissance Unit 13 / SS Mountain Reconnaissance Unit 13
SS Armored Reconnaissance Unit
Croatian SS Cycle Battalion
Croatian SS Engineer Battalion / SS Mountain Engineer Battalion 13
Croatian SS Motorcycle Rifle Battalion
SS Division supply troops
SS Division Supply Leader 13
Supply Regiment Staff 13
SS Administrative Battalion 13
SS Storekeeping Battalion 13
SS Medical Battalion 13
SS Mountain Veterinary Company 13

(Division troops — such as the field police troop or the Croatian Repair Unit 13 — with SS number 13)

d) War Service

Between 1944 and 1945 the division saw service exclusively in the Southeast — and in fact, it was first transported to Yugoslavia and active in the northeastern section of Bosnia, where its task was securing the region between the Bosut and the Save. Then it went into combat against Tito's partisan bands near Bijeljina, Koraj and in the Celic area, as well as near Rahic, Ratkovic and Mitrovica. Then came the securing of the mining area of Ugljevic on the Janja and in the Janja region, Operation "Maibaum", fighting against partisan bands southeast of Tuzla, in the area west of Zvornik and near Gornaja, Tuzla and Derventa. [25]

What happened then?

"The mysterious action of the SS "Handschar" Division in Hungary and later in Vienna still needs clarification," wrote George H. Stein: "Hausser, who commanded army groups in the North and West in the last months of the war, had no personal knowledge of the events in the Southeast and was therefore misled by the security measures of the OKW. At the beginning of 1945 it was decided to transfer the elite 16th SS Panzergrenadier Division "Reichsführer-SS" from northern Italy to the hard-pressed Hungarian front. In order to deceive the enemy, "Reichsführer-SS" was disguised as the non-existent 13th Waffen-SS Mountain Division "Handschar" . . . It was the "Reichsführer-SS" wolf in the sheep's clothing of the "Handschar" that fought on the Drau, then north of the Plattensee and finally in Vienna." [26]

e) Division Commanders

SS Standartenführer Herbert von Oberwurzer 1943
SS Brigadeführer and Generalmajor of the Waffen-SS
Karl-Gustav Sauberzweig 1943-June 1944
SS Brigadeführer and Generalmajor of the Waffen-SS
Desiderius Hampel June 1944-end

f) Insignia

Instead of shoulder patches, the members of this division wore a patch with the Croatian coat of arms on the left upper sleeve of their uniforms.

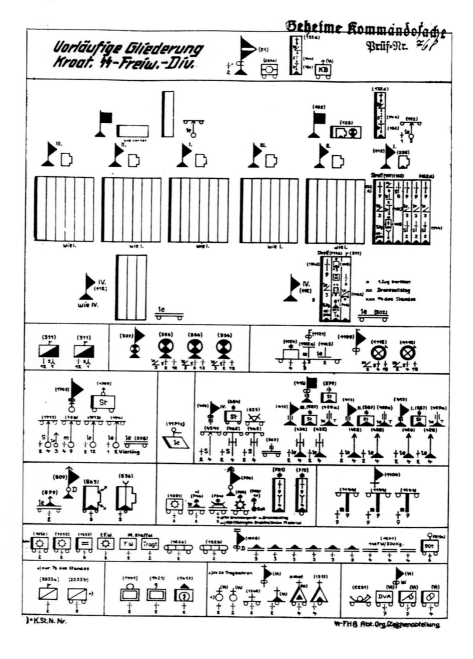

g) Division Emblem

The Arabian sword called the "Handschar" was worn on the right collar patch (instead of the SS Sigrune) and also carried on vehicles as their tactical symbol.

4. The 21st Waffen-SS Mountain Division "Skanderbeg"

a) Origin

This mountain division with the Albanian number 1 was established by an order of April 17, 1944, in the Pac-Pristina-Prizren region of northern Albania on May 1, by means of transferring the Albanians serving in the 13th Waffen-SS Mountain Division "Handschar", and thus consisted exclusively of Moslems. Its units, originally established as Mountain Jäger Regiments 1 and 2 and only in September as Mountain Jäger Regiments 1 and 2, bore the Albanian numbers 1 and 2 after being assembled on October 11, 1944, and had three mountain Jäger battalions each. According to Tessin, the division was not yet fully established. In November and December 1944 the records list only the Regimental Group "Skanderbeg." In January 1945, when the Albanians were discharged, the German cadre personnel were absorbed into the SS Mountain Jäger Regiment 14 of the 7th SS Volunteer Mountain Division "Prinz Eugen." [27]

b) Structure

Waffen-SS Mountain Jäger Regiment 50
Waffen-SS Mountain Jäger Regiment 51
SS (Mountain) Reconnaissance Unit 21
SS (Mountain) Panzerjäger Unit 21
Waffen-SS Mountain Artillery Regiment 21
SS Mountain Engineer Battalion 21
SS Mountain Intelligence Unit 21
SS Mountain Replacement Battalion 21
SS Assault Gun Unit "Skanderbeg"
SS Medical Unit 21
SS Storekeeping Battalion 21
(Division troops — such as the Commander of the SS Mountain Supply Troops 21 — with SS number 21)

c) War Service

The division saw service exclusively in the Balkans in 1944-1945 — beginning at the end of June 1944 with anti-partisan action in the Djakovica region, in the Mokra Gora west and northwest of Pac, and near Hadzovici and Algina Reci. In mid-November the Regimental Group "Skanderbeg" was transferred out of the region of Pristina into that of Kraljevo. Then it saw service in the Uzice-Rogacica region and eastward of Sarajevo near Podromanija. Its withdrawal combat took it in a northerly direction into the Janja-Bijeljina area and then into the Save sector near Brcko. Here it was absorbed into the 7th SS Volunteer Mountain Division "Prinz Eugen." [28]

d) Division Commanders

SS Birgadeführer and Generalmajor of the Waffen-SS
August Schmidhuber
SS Obersturmbannführer Graf (i.V.)

e) Insignia
Instead of a shoulder patch, the members of the 21st Waffen-SS Mountain Division "Skanderbeg" wore a patch with the Albanian double eagle on the left upper sleeve of their uniforms.

f) Division Symbol
The Albanian double eagle.

Waffen-SS Mountain Division "Skanderbeg" (Albanian No. 1)

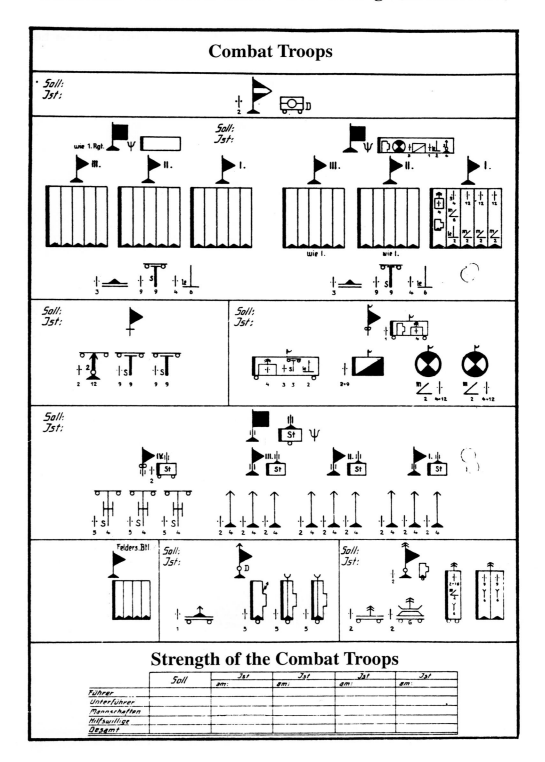

Combat Troops

Strength of the Combat Troops

	Soll	Jst am:	Jst am:	Jst am:	Jst am:
Führer					
Unterführer					
Mannschaften					
Hilfswillige					
Gesamt					

Waffen-SS Mountain Division "Skanderbeg" (Albanian No. 1)

Supply Troops

Soll:
Jst:

Soll:
Jst:

Soll: Jst: | Soll: Jst: | Soll: Jst: | Soll: Jst: | Soll: Jst:

Strength of the Supply Troops

	Soll	Jst am:	Jst am:	Jst am:	Jst am:
Führer					
Unterführer					
Mannschaften					
Hilfswillige					
Gesamt					

Total Strength of the Waffen-SS Mountain Division "Skanderbeg"

	Soll	Jst am:	Jst am:	Jst am:	Jst am:
Führer					
Unterführer					
Mannschaften					
Hilfswillige					
Gesamt					

Waffen	Soll	Jst am:	Jst am:	Jst am:	Jst am:
Pistolen					
m. P.					
Gewehre					
le. M.G.					
s. M.G.					
m. Gr. W.					
s. Gr. W.					
Fm. W.					
Werfer					
s. Panz. Buchs.					
3,7 cm Pak					
5 cm Pak					
7,5 cm Pak					
7,5 cm Pak (Sf)					
le. J G.					
s. J. G.					
2 cm Flak					
2 cm Flak (Vierl)					
3,7 cm Flak					
8,8 cm Flak					
Geb Gesch. 36					
le. F.H.					
le. F.H. (mot Z)					
s. F.H. (mot. Z)					
10,5 cm K (mot Z)					

Pz.-Fahrzeuge	Soll	Jst am:	Jst am:	Jst am:	Jst am:

Pferde	Soll	Jst am:	Jst am:	Jst am:	Jst am:
Reitpferde					
Bergreitpferde					
Tragtiere					
Packpferde					
le. Zugpferde					
schw. Zugpferde					
schwste Zugpferde					

gez. Zeichenabt. SS-FHA Org. Abt. Iª/II.

31

5. The 23rd Waffen-SS Mountain Division "Kama"

a) Origin

The establishment of this Waffen-SS Mountain Division with the Croatian number 2, and made up of Croatian nationals, began with an order of June 17, 1944 and took place in the Save-Bosna-Spreca-Drina area of Croatia. Just seven days later, on June 24, the assembly area was moved to southern Hungary, to the former assembly area of the 18th SS Volunteer Panzergrenadier Division "Horst Wessel."

According to Tessin, "the establishment, to which the 13th SS Mountain Division "Handschar" had to provide one battery as a personal unit for every unit of the artillery regiment, had to be finished by December 31, 1944. By an order of 9/24/1944, the division then being formed was disbanded, all Moslem officers, junior officers and men, with 1000 carbineers were immediately sent to SS General Command IX in Croatia and absorbed into the Waffen-SS Mountain Division "Handschar." The remaining personnel and all materials were to be kept ready for the formation of an SS grenadier division in Hungary." [29] This was the 31st SS Volunteer Panzergrenadier Division "Böhmen-Mähren."

b) Structure

Waffen-SS Mountain Jäger Regiment 55 (Croatian No. 3)
Waffen-SS Mountain Jäger Regiment 56 (Croatian No. 4)
Waffen-SS Mountain Artillery Regiment 23
SS Reconnaissance Unit 23
SS Panzerjäger Unit 23
SS Flak Unit 23
SS Engineer Battalion 23
SS Mountain Intelligence Unit 23
SS Replacement Battalion 23
SS Administrative Troop Unit 23

(Division troops — such as the Commander SS Division Supply Troops 23 — with the SS number 23)

c) Division Commander

SS Standartenführer Hellmuth Raithel

d) Division Symbol

The sun symbol.

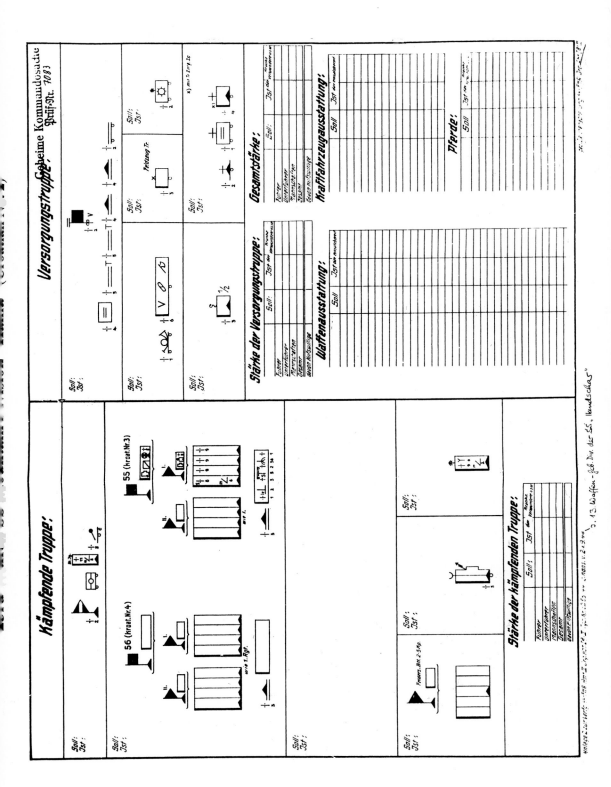

33

6. The 24th Waffen-SS Mountain Division "Karstjäger"

a) Origin

On orders of July 18, 1944, the "Karstjäger" Division was established on August 1 in the realm of the Higher SS and Police Leader of the "Adriatic Coastland", the Carinthian Gauleiter Dr. Friedrich Rainer, of members of the peoples and ethnic groups living in that area, and with German command personnel. In any case, it never attained a strength of more than 2000 men. "The SS Karst-Jäger Battalion (also referred to as the Pol. Volunteer Battalion Karstwehr) established in the winter of 1942-1943, became the first battalion of the first regiment. The division was to attain the full structure of a mountain division with two Jäger regiments (59 and 60), reconnaissance unit, Panzerjäger unit, artillery regiment with four units, engineer battery, intelligence unit, replacement battalion, units of division supply troops and administrative troops. . . . Since filling the division proved to be impossible, it was reorganized, by order of 12/5/1944, into a Waffen-SS Mountain (Karstjäger) Brigade, which was to be established by 1/30/1945 by the commander of the Waffen-SS in Italy. . . . In February 1945 the brigade was renamed the 24th Waffen-SS Mountain (Karstjäger) Division. [30]

b) Structure

    Waffen-SS Mountain Jäger Regiment 59
    Waffen-SS Mountain Jäger Regiment 60
    Waffen-SS Mountain Artillery Regiment 24
    SS Mountain Reconnaissance Unit 24
    SS Mountain Panzerjäger Unit 24 (1 Co.)
    SS Mountain Engineer Battalion (1 Co.)
    SS Mountain Intelligence Unit 24
    SS Replacement Battalion 24
(Division troops — such as Division Supply Troop 24 — with SS number 24)

c) War Service

The Karstjäger were selected for service in the roadless and rugged chalk mountains of southeastern Europe, more particularly the boundary areas between Slovenia and Croatia, and the Friaul and Udine, to fight against partisan bands.

Combat in the mountainous region, with its bizarre rock formations, extensive hills and thick forests, required very special training, which was carried out in the Salzkammergut and in the Franconian Alb. [31]

The Waffen-SS Mountain Brigade "Karstjäger" saw service in the three-country area of Yugoslavia, Italy and Carinthia, as well as in Istria, against the numerous partisan bands. In 1945 it fought partisans in Italy, in the area of Tarvisio and the upper Isonzo Valley, as well as in the eastern part of the rugged Julian Alps. Its last action came in the wooded area around Ternova on the Isonzo. In May 1945 to SS Brigade capitulated on the Isonzo and became British prisoners of war.

d) Division Commanders

Unknown.

e) Division Emblem

A stylized Thyr-rune with an arrow on either side of the shaft.

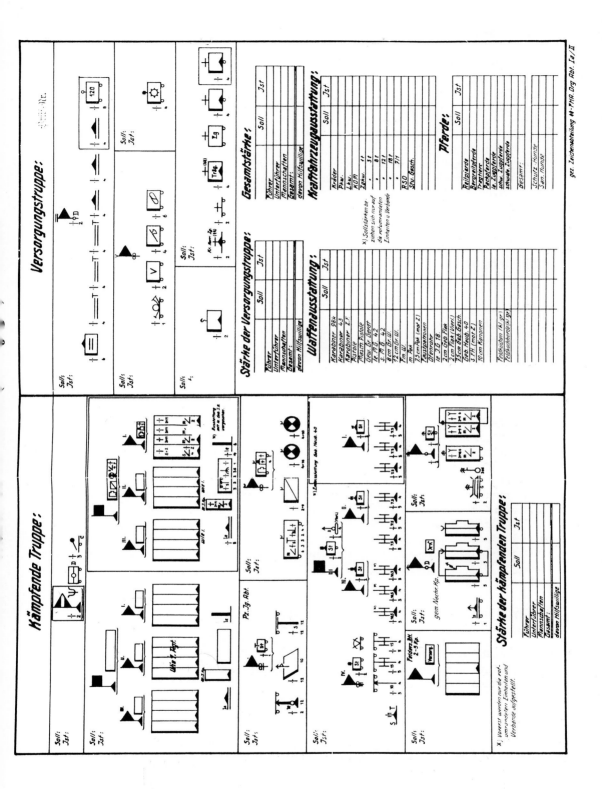

IV. The Named Groups of the SS Mountain Troops

1. The SS Mountain Jäger Regiment 11 "Reinhard Heydrich"

First its pre-history: The **SS-Totenkopf-Standarte 6** was formed in Prague on September 12, 1939, of men taken from the four older Totenkopf-Standarten. In October 1939 it was partially transferred to Danzig and Bromberg, where the SS-Totenkopf-Standarte 9 came into being. It was reorganized in Prague and transferred from there to southern Norway on April 27, 1940. The III. Sturmbann, though, had remained in Prague and become part of the new SS-Totenkopf-Standarte 14. [32]

The **SS Infantry Regiment 6** (mot) existed since February 25, 1941 — and now wore the Sigrunes of the SS instead of the death's-head of the Totenkopf units on the collars of its uniforms. On June 4, 1942 this regiment, located in Prague, received a message from the Führer, transmitted from his headquarters by radio, giving it the name "Reinhard Heydrich", or "RH" for short, which was also given to the SS Mountain Jäger Regiment 6. [33]

Reinhard Heydrich assumed the leadership of the political police, later that of the "Geheime Staatspolizeiamt" (Gestapo), in Prussia during the course of the equalization of the German states, working in close cooperation with Heinrich Himmler, in 1933-34. After Himmler had taken over the leadership of the entire German police in 1936, Heydrich, serving as chief of the "Sicherheitspolizei" (Security Police) and the SD, and since 1939 as the leader of the Reich Security Headquarters (RSHA), gained a leading position in the Third Reich. Empowered by Goering with carrying out the "final solution" of the Jewish question, he conducted the Wannsee Conference in January 1942. Since September 1941 Heydrich was also the executive Reich protector of Bohemia and Moravia. On June 5, 1942 he was assassinated in Prague, the attack being prepared by the Czech Government-in-exile in London. Thereupon the SS undertook a reprisal action against the village of Lidice, in which the assassins were said to have found shelter.

Cuff Title

2. The SS Mountain Jäger Regiment 12 "Michael Geissmair"

Its pre-history: the **SS-Totenkopf-Standarte 7** was founded at Brno on September 12, 1939, of men from the four old Totenkopf-Standarten, and transferred from Brno to southern Norway on April 27, 1940. The II. Sturmbann stayed behind in Brno and joined the disbanding SS-Totenkopf-Standarte 9. It was replaced in the regiment by the I. Totenkopf-Rekrutenstandarte from Klagenfurt. On September 12, 1940 came the order to motorize. [34]

The **SS Infantry Regiment 7** (mot) existed since February 25, 1941. The death's-head emblem on the collars of the uniforms was now replaced by the Sigrune of the Waffen-SS.

The **SS Mountain Jäger Regiment 7** came into being with the restructuring of the SS Mountain Division "Nord" in September 1942. The regiment was formed anew of the staff of the old unit and the three SS Mountain Jäger Battalions I-III, which had been organized in Wildflecken since that spring. When the Waffen-SS units were numbered sequentially on October 22, 1943, the regiment was given the name of **SS Mountain Jäger Regiment 12**. On June 20, 1944, it was given the name "Michael Gaissmair." [35]

Michael Gaissmair, toll collector and scribe of the Prince-Bishop of Brixen, led the Tyrolean peasants in the peasant's rebellion of 1525-26. After the rebellion ended, he wrote a "Tyrolean State Order" that foresaw a new order of state and society — and portrayed a classless society of the future, a free people's state without power and oppression. In particular, he foresaw the foundation of a Christian-democratic peasant's republic in Tyrol. The "Peasant Rebel" was murdered in Padua in 1532.

Cuff Title

3. The SS Volunteer Mountain Jäger Regiment 13 "Artur Phleps"

This regiment was created on October 22, 1943 by the renaming of the **SS Volunteer Mountain Jäger Regiment 1**. The name "Artur Phleps" was given to it in the autumn of 1944, in memory of the well-known SS Obergruppenführer and General of the Waffen-SS.

Artur Phleps was already a highly decorated general staff officer of the Imperial and Royal Army in World War I. After spending some time with the Romanian mountain troops, Phleps, who came from Siebenbürgen, asked his country for permission to join the German Wehrmacht when war broke out with Russia. When his request was granted, he volunteered for the Waffen-SS. On January 13, 1942, Phleps, now an SS Brigadeführer and Major General of the Waffen-SS, was given the task of forming, as he saw fit, a powerful division of Serbian ethnic Germans in the Banat region of Serbia. Thus arose the later 7th SS Volunteer Mountain Division "Prinz Eugen." In the spring of 1943 — decorated with the Knight's Cross and promoted to SS Obergruppenführer and General of the Waffen-SS — he was named commanding general and charged with the establishment and leadership of the V. SS Mountain Corps. Thus he took command of the "Prinz Eugen" Division as well as the 13th Waffen-SS Mountain Division "Handschar" and three army divisions. Artur Phleps was killed during a scouting trip in the front area of the Romanian Banat on September 21, 1944.

Cuff Title

4. The SS Volunteer Mountain Jäger Regiment 14 "Skanderbeg"

This regiment came into being on October 22, 1943, with the renaming of the **SS Volunteer Mountain Jäger Regiment 2**. The name "Skanderbeg" was given to it in the autumn of 1944 in memory of the Albanian freedom fighter.

Skanderbeg was actually Georg Kastriota, an Albanian prince and freedom fighter. He used trickery to capture the mountain fortress of Kruje and was proclaimed General-Captain of Albania. He led many successful campaigns against the Turks and, with Venetian support, defended Albanian independence for the rest of his life.

[Note: I believe "Skanderbeg" originally meant "Alexander the Great" and that a large lake in the Balkans was named after him. I suspect this man then took the name, either from Alexander or the lake, as his pseudonym.]

Cuff Title

5. The SS Ski Jäger Battalion "Norge"

The SS Ski (Jäger) Battalion "Norge" must not be forgotten. Formed of Danish, Norwegian and Swedish volunteers, it was subordinated to the 6th SS Mountain Division "Nord." It saw service exclusively in the Finnish-Russian war zone and was disbanded on December 1, 1944.

Cuff Title

6. The SS-og-Polit Company

The word "Polit" here does not stand for politics or party — has often been claimed — but for police. Members of this company wore shoulder patches with the lettering "Frw. Legion Norwegen."

Cuff Title

V. The Mountain Jäger Training and Replacement Battalions

Like the SS Panzer-Grenadier replacement and training battalions, the replacement and training battalions of the Waffen-SS mountain troops were generally linked with the SS mountain divisions of the same "house number." This means that the mountain divisions of the Waffen-SS could normally call on the SS Mountain Jäger Training and Replacement Battalions 6, 7, 13, 21 and 24 for new manpower.

1. The SS Mountain Jäger Replacement Battalion
This battalion was founded in Trautenau on March 15, 1942, from the SS Replacement Battalion "Nord" — formerly of Wehlau, East Prussia — as the training and replacement battalion of the 6th SS Mountain Division "Nord."

2. The SS Mountain Jäger Training and Replacement Battalion 6
This battalion was organized in Hallein, near Salzburg, on May 10, 1943, from the SS Mountain Jäger Replacement Battalion "Nord", which had been established on September 6, 1940. In January 1945 parts of it joined Volunteer Regiment 32/

3. The SS Mountain Jäger Training and Replacement Battalion 7
This battalion was created in Pantschowa, near Belgrade, in May of 1943, out of the SS Mountain Jäger Replacement Battalion 'Prinz Eugen'', which had been founded in 1942. On November 1, 1943 it was transferred to Weisskirchen (Werschetz) in the Banat. In June 1944 the Replacement and Training Battalion was separated, but it was reunited in September, and it was transferred to Gradiska in northern Italy on May 15, 1944, and then to Görz in 1945.

4. The SS Mountain Jäger Training and Replacement Battalion 13
This battalion was founded at Neuhammer, Silesia, in November 1943, assembled at Brcko, Croatia, in 1944, and transferred to Leoben on the Mur on October 1, 1944. This SS battalion was at first, according to the original plans, only the training and replacement unit for the 13th Waffen-SS Mountain Division "Handschar", but later it also served the 23rd Waffen-SS Mountain Division "Kama" and the General Command of the IX. Waffen-SS Mountain Corps. In addition, when the 9th Mountain Division, formerly the "Battle Group Semmering" or "Battle Group Raithel", was established in 1945, the SS Mountain Jäger Training and Replacement Battalion 13 became one of the supporting pillars of this large-scale mountain unit of the German Wehrmacht. [36]

The Waffen-SS Mountain Jäger School near Neustift in the Stubai Valley.

Photos

VI. Training

Above: Swearing in; below: Marching out, and (right), grenade-launcher training.

Waffen-SS mountain soldiers being sworn in.

The Reichsführer-SS visits the troops. At far right is SS Gruppenführer and Generalleutnant of the Waffen-SS Artur Phleps.

Radiomen in the high mountains.

Outdoor instruction.

Outdoor discussion.

Himmler inspecting the equipment of Waffen-SS mountain troops.

Medical corps training.

Himmler and General of the Waffen-SS Phleps (right) visiting the troops.

Himmler inspecting Waffen-SS mountain artillery.

Weapon inspection.

Orientation in the mountains.

51

VII. The Scandinavian Theater

A scouting troop in Finland.

View of the Liinehameri Fjord, with a fishing village in the rear.

Generaloberst Dietl surrounded by nurses. As commander of the 20th Mountain Army, the 6th SS Mountain Division "Nord" was under his command in Finland.

Left: General Siilasuvo (III. Finnish Army Corps) with the commander of the 6th SS Mountain Division, Generalmajor of the Waffen-SS Kleinheisterkamp. Right: Commander of the 6th SS Mountain Division "Nord", General of the Waffen-SS Krüger.

Sea transport of the 6th SS Mountain Division "Nord" along the Norwegian coast . . .

. . . on relatively small steamers.

View of the Lofoten Islands . . .

. . . and of "Reichsstrasse 50" along the Varanger-Fjord.

The staff of Battle Group "Nord", which soon became the staff of the 6th SS Mountain Division "Nord."

Situation conference with the commander of the 6th SS Mountain Division, SS Brigadenführer and Generalmajor Matthias Kleinheisterkamp (with mosquito net).

Long-range scouting troop of the 6th SS Mountain Division "Nord" before setting out on a five-day march to the Murman Road.

A member of the 6th SS Mountain Division "Nord."

A makeshift footbridge over a brook.

Building a corduroy road over swampy terrain.

Mail and food are brought forward.

Panzerjäger of the 6th SS Mountain Division "Nord" near Salla.

Left: Loyal companions, beast of burden and leader.

Right: As well as food, equipment and ammunition had to be moved forward in this manner.

Right: An observation post of an advanced observer in the SS Mountain Artillery.

Below: A barrack bunker on the Kiestinki Front.

A Waffen-SS scouting troop before the Gudrun Position.

The bridge near Schjana on the Kuusamo-Kiestinki road. The river joins the Top-See to the south with the Pja-See to the north.

A bunker in a snow-covered landscape.

A sentry in deep snow.

Above and below: Military cemetery of the 6th SS Mountain Division "Nord" on the "May-Way" east of Kiestinki.

VIII. The Balkan Theater

This photo from the Balkans, clearly shows the difficult terrain.

At right is a 2 cm Flak gun of the 7th SS Volunteer Mountain Division "Prinz Eugen."

Mountain Jäger of the Waffen-SS on their way to the front.

Here again, the same unit with its beasts of burden.

The division commander of the 7th SS Volunteer Mountain Division "Prinz Eugen", Generalleutnant of the Waffen-SS Phleps, informs the commander of SS Mountain Jäger Regiment 2 (Obersturmbannführer Schmidhuber).

Generalleutnant of the Waffen-SS Phleps with General of the Infantry von Unruh (OKW) in front of a sentry post. At left on the post house is the emblem of the "Prinz Eugen" Division.

Motorcycle riflemen of the 7th SS Volunteer Mountain Division "Prinz Eugen" (note division emblem on the sidecars) in a Bosnian city.

Motorcycle riflemen of the "Prinz Eugen" Division marching during Kapaonik operations.

Action in northeastern Bosnia.

On the way to new action.

Into battle for the first time.

Pursuing the retreating enemy.

Moving forward on undriveable paths, supplies can be carried only by beasts of burden.

Marching into the chalk mountains.

In the winter, runners are attached to the wagon wheels.

Between actions there is time for much-needed ski training.

Reichsführer-SS Himmler and other high SS officials visited the 7th SS Volunteer Mountain Division "Prinz Eugen." At the far right below is the commander of this division, Generalleutnant of the Waffen-SS Artur Phleps.

Set up and secure support points — a constant task.

Support points and gun nests (below) are secured with light machine guns.

Training continues ceaselessly, including drill and (below) a guard moving out.

Here General of the Infantry von Unruh (OKW) visits the SS Mountain Division "Prinz Eugen."

Standing at right is the Commanding General of the V. SS Mountain Corps, General of the Waffen-SS Phleps.

A Christmas party for the 7th SS Mountain Division "Prinz Eugen."

Below: After Italy fell, assault boats were used to occupy Adriatic islands populated by Italians.

A mountain gun in an open firing position.

The swastika flag on the road shows the Luftwaffe that the guns ahead — presumably in direct aim — are in action.

The blown-up bridge over the Korana at Sluni. Units of the "Prinz Eugen" Division saw action here.

A sudden snowfall threatened to bring operations to a stop near Petrovak.

84

Great demands are made on men and animals in snow-covered terrain.

A heavy eight-wheel "ADGZ" armored car. These vehicles, taken over in the Anschluss with Austria in 1938, saw much service with the Waffen-SS in the Balkans. This one is camouflaged for winter.

Generalleutnant of the Waffen-SS Phleps (Commander, 7th SS Mountain Division "Prinz Eugen") with the commander of the Italian "Marche" Division, Major General Amido, in Mostar.

SS Brigadeführer and Generalmajor of the Waffen-SS Otto Kumm, bearer of the Knight's Cross with oak leaves and swords, Commander of the "Prinz Eugen" Division as of 8/1/ 1944.

A look up the Nare Valley near an old Roman bridge in Mostar.

Nevesinje, the town that served as the "Prinz Eugen" Division's command post in Operation "Schwarz", May 1943.

Communication with Italian forces during Operation "Schwarz."

SS-Stubaf. Dietsche, Kdr. II./2 im Gespräch mit einem
Brigadekommandanten der Cetniks.

And contact with the Cetniks, who were also involved.

Captured French tanks in action with the 7th Volunteer Mountain Division "Prinz Eugen."

This 2 cm quadruple gun was also used by the Waffen-SS mountain troops.

After a long march in rough country on a hot day, every exhausted man falls asleep on the grass at once.

Cattle are not only food reserves, but also beasts of burden.

After the battle, wounded animals are also given medical care.

A captured heavy machine gun in action near Presjeka.

Above and below: The mountain artillery of the Waffen-SS in action near Niksic.

First aid treatment on the battlefield.

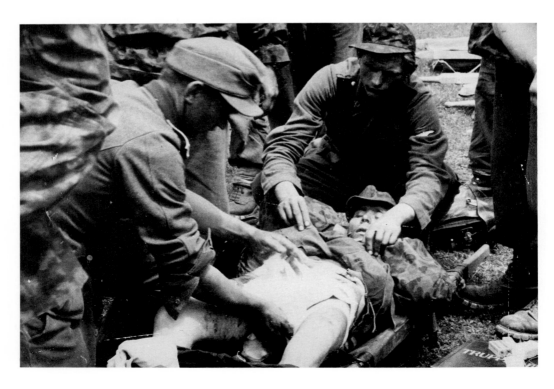

Wounded men are carried away by their comrades . . .

. . . and then by the Medical Corps, which brings them to a main dressing station for further medical care.

A main dressing station (H.V.Pl.) near Niksic.

The Commander of the 7th SS Volunteer Mountain Division, Artur Phleps, with the leader of the surgical unit, SS Hauptsturmführer Dr. Kirchner.

Slightly wounded men — treated by Red Cross nurses — wait for transportation.

Badly wounded men were also carried by transport planes on their return trips.

The commander of the German troops in Croatia (General Lüters) in Podgorica on May 22, 1943.
Above: At the airoort; in the center is Oberleutnant Kurt Waldheim. Below, reviewing the Company of Honor of the 7th SS Volunteer Mountain Division "Prinz Eugen."

Another photo taken during General Lüters' visit. In front are SS Gruppenführer and Generalleutnant of the Waffen-SS Phleps and Ecc. Roncaglia.

A truck carries members of the "Prinz Eugen" Division through the Italian support point of Bileca.

A photo of Himmler's visit to the 7th SS Volunteer Mountain Division "Prinz Eugen", with SS Gruppenführer and Generalleutnant of the Waffen-SS Phleps in front.

SS Obersturmbannführer Bayer (leader of Unit VI) visits the division headquarters in Niksic. At right is Otto Kumm.

Above and below: A regimental commander (note pennant on car) in a car with the emblem of the 7th SS Volunteer Mountain Division "Prinz Eugen" on a scouting trip.

Arrival (presumably of the artillery) in Mostar.

A light infantry gun in firing position near Lukowo.

Trackless country.

Division fuel depot.

Father and son — Artur and Dr. Reinhart Phleps — both of the 7th SS Mountain Division. The father (left) is already an SS Obergruppenführer and General of the Waffen-SS.

This photo shows a visit of the commander of German troops in Croatia, General Lüters, at Gacko.

Bogumil graves.

Another bogumil grave near Kifino-Selo.

A look at the Bandnj from the command post of SS Mountain Jäger Regiment 1 on the Stoca Heights.

In the hills there were scarcely any large plants, and camouflage was very difficult.

After Italy surrendered (secret armistice, September 1943), there were brief battles between Germans and Italians in the Balkans. Here are weapons and equipment that the Italians abandoned in Dubrovnik.

This is a prisoner-of-war camp, where thousands of Italians were kept after their disarmament.

From left to right: Stubaf. Jurey, Brif. von Oberkamp (Commander of the "Prinz Eugen" Division, 7/3/43-2/1/44), Gruf. Phleps, Staf. Schmidhuber, Ostubaf. Wagner, during a visit to the Alpine training of SS Mountain Jäger Regiment 2 in Sitomislic.

The cemetery of the 7th SS Volunteer Mountain Division "Prinz Eugen" at Niksic.

A speech to volunteers of the Waffen-SS mountain troops.

Members of SS Mountain Jäger Regiment 2 of the "Prinz Eugen" Division.

A bridge built by the Waffen-SS mountain engineers in the Balkans.

The general observes his division on the march.

Members of the SS Mountain Communications Troop in the highlands of Rakita.

The supply train fords the Sutjeska River.

The troops can or must deal with good (above), bad, and trackless (below) terrain.

Above and below: Generaloberst Dr. Rendulic visits the V. SS Mountain Corps. As of 6/25/1944 he was the commander of the 20th Mountain Army.

In the squares of all the cities and towns in Croatia, these recruiting placards for the Croatian Waffen-SS Mountain Division appeared.

Reichsführer-SS Himmler with the 13th Waffen-SS Mountain Division "Handschar." At right is the division commander, SS Brigadeführer Sauberzweig.

Commanding General Phleps of the V. SS Mountain Corps visits the "Handschar." He still wears the emblem and stripe of the "Prinz Eugen" Division on his sleeve.

The Great Mufti of Jerusalem visits the 13th Waffen-SS Mountain Division "Handschar."

Here he reviews an honor guard of the division.

Moslem volunteers at morning roll call.

Soldiers of the 13th Waffen-SS Mountain Division "Handschar." The field-gray fez was worn in action.

A "Handschar" sentry guards parked VW amphibious vehicles.

Members of the "Handschar" Division during training.

This photo shows the different fez colors: field-gray at right, left and center red for parades etc.

A mountain Jäger tank of the 13th Waffen-SS Mountain Division "Handschar" in action against partisans.

The "ADGZ" (Austro-Daimler-Puch Works AG) armored car, taken over from the Austrian Bundesheer in 1938, in service with the 7th SS Volunteer Mountain Division "Prinz Eugen."

Below: Their best-known division commander in action.

IX. Documents

FOREWORD

From the many documents still available, these have been chosen as being of particular interest.

33-Division North
Commander

Division Command Post, 6/23/1941

Div.Gef.Std., den 23.6.1941.

To the Commanding General of the XXXVI. Army Corps
General of the Cavalry Pelge

On the basis of constantly repeated personal observations of the troop units of the SS I. R. 7 located at the front in the last few days, as well as of the mass of the Division, which has now arrived after much delay, I respectfully offer my observation that I am of the opinion that the level of training of the troops turned over to me is so bad that the responsibility for their used cannot be assumed.

I respectfully ask the General that the Division, after its first task, which cannot be changed, be given the time and opportunity to go to a troop training camp and make up everything that it is lacking.

The tactical training of the commanders, as also of the mass of the leaders, is fully insufficient. The single combat training of the individual men, like the training of the groups, is completely insufficient. The supply troops are capable of doing their duty only under the greatest difficulties.

I respectfully report to the Commanding General in order to clarify the situation regarding the actual value of these troops in combat.

The Division Commander

H

SS Brigadeführer and Major General

The answer from the General stated:

High Command XXXVI HQ,

0083

June 24, 1941

To the Commander of the SS Division Nord
Brigadeführer and Major General Demelhuber

I thank you for your report of 6/23 and the frank description of the level of training and the evaluation of the troop units subordinate to you.

Although I share your concern in reference to the value of the troops and the achievements to be expected of them, I am nevertheless convinced that the SS division, under your clear and energetic leadership, will carry out the task intended for them in the planned combat.

With the good human material and the high level of readiness for action, good will should equalize many weaknesses.

General of the Cavalry

SS-Division Nord   St.Qu., June 30, 1941
Unit Ia No. 9/41 3.Kdos. Three Copies   Secret Command Material

Situation Report of the SS Division Nord

Unit: SS Division Nord
Subordinate to: General Command XXXVI

1) Lacking on Day of Report:

a) Lack of Personnel

	Full	Present	Lack
Officers	361	306	55
Junior Officers	1575	1159	316
Enlisted Men	8230	8048	182

b) Lacking Weapons and Equipment
    1) Pz.B.40 58
    2) l.Gr.W. 36 (5 cm) 10
    3) s.Gr.W. 34 (8 cm) 12
    4) l.J.G. 18 12
    5) 2 cm Flak 30 2
    6) MS-Gerät (Mine detector) Köln 40 18
    7) kl. Air Compressor for Engineers 6
    8) Set of Boring Tools for Engineers 6
    9) Dough-kneading Trailer for Bakery 1

Of the available weapons, the following percentages are Czech:
    Side arms   60%
    Rifles   40%
    Pistols   75%
    Light Machine Guns   95%
    Heavy Machine Guns   85%
All weapons are ready for use in the field.

c) Motor Vehicles
    1) Light Motorcycles .... —
    2) Medium Motorcycles 65
    3) Heavy Motorcycles 148
    4) Sidecars 124

5. Medium Off-road Cars 101
6. Light Trucks 109
7. Light Off-road Trucks 33
8. Medium Off-road Trucks 9
9. Heavy Off-road Trucks 1

2. <u>Losses and other lacks since last report</u>:
   None; this is first report.

3. <u>Replacements received since last report</u>:
   None, this is first report.

4. <u>Commander's Evaluation</u>:

On June 17, 1941, I took command of the SS Division Nord. The division has been assembled quickly very recently, and the artillery was added to it at the last possible moment.

The very first impression showed that the basic training of the troops — individual combat training — is very weak, and thus the unit training is fully nonexistent.

The leadership and troops do not deserve any blame, for they were given no opportunity to do this carefully and under experienced leadership. The majority of the commanders and company chiefs are reserve officers with very little or absolutely no troop or war experience in modern warfare. The battalion officers' abilities are in no way sufficient and only approximate the leadership of modern infantry combat with bound weapons to some extent.

The artillery fired only once at Jüterbog and never along with the infantry. Likewise, the infantry has never had the opportunity to drill with the artillery.

The antitank forces have not fired live ammunition; the same is true of the light grenade launchers, and to a great degree the flak batteries as well.

Drills with mixed bands have never taken place.

The troops have not been trained for combat action.

The supply unit of the division was assembled in Stettin at the last minute, and its command does not live up to the responsibilities which it must take to supply the fighting troops.

Motorization has been made difficult by the fact that a variety of types are present, and even in the individual units no uniformity of type could be achieved.

Obtaining spare parts is difficult. The towing tractors of the artillery do not live up to the requirements of a German motorized division (being French Somua and Unic types).

The infantry regiments have only one light J.G. platoon.

The division staff must be trained only now before an attack.

The manpower material is good, in part very good. The junior officers must be trained. The specialist training is very limited.

I have already reported this state of affairs to the commanding general.

The division will be fully prepared for action when it is given the opportunity, as was and is the case for all newly formed units, to be trained for two or three months at a good troop training facility.

Division Commander

SS Brigadeführer
and Generalmajor

Recipients:

1st Copy = General Command XXXVI
2nd Copy = Command Office, Waffen-SS
3rd Copy = z.d.A. Unit Ia - g.Kdos.

One can imagine that the replying general, who certainly shared the considerable concern of the division commander, must also have felt the pressure of strict orders from the AOK Norway.

Reichssicherheitshauptamt

Nachrichten-Uebermittlung

	Aufgenommen			Raum für Eingangsstempel		Befördert		
Zeit	Tag	Monat	Jahr		Zeit	Tag	Monat	Jahr
von		durch		1943	**Der Reichsführer SS**			
				19	Adjutantur *S4/43,4v*			
N.-U. Nr.				Telegramm — Funkspruch — Fernschreiben				
				Fernspruch				

Command Material VST RFSS Berlin   0016 19/2 43 2210 == KOE =

SECRET COMMAND MATERIAL

SS VOLUNTEER DIVISION "PRINZ EUGEN"

To Reichsführer SS:

Report results of my talk in Agram yesterday with emissary

Kasche, Foreign Minister Lorkovic and Colonel Funk, representa-

tive of General Laise-Horstenau, regarding Moslem SS division.

Croatian government welcomes establishment, recruiting by

Germans unwanted for reasons of domestic and foreign policy.

Poglavnik puts value on name of Ustascha Division, Croatian

uniforms and insignia of rank, and as much Croatian language of command as possible. Formation in the country is desired for

security reasons. Croats can immediately provide 6000 Ustascha

volunteers. In addition, the support of the Moslem leader of north-

east Bosnia is assured in the providing of volunteers. Great diffi-

culties will be caused by the provision of officer and junior officer

personnel. This SS Ustascha Division of Croatia, as the designa-

tion is desired, cannot be spoken of as SS, but is rather a Croatian

unit set up with the help of the SS.

Standartenführer Dengel is empowered from here to clarify all

questions about establishment in advance with the staff of the

commanding general in Agram, and then to establish the personnel

lists with the help of Croatian government agencies. The division

Reichssicherheitshauptamt

will, in fact, be set up like the Prinz Eugen, with the exception of special units or

| Aufgenommen | | | | Raum für Eingangsstempel | | Befördert | | | |
| Zeit | Tag | Monat | Jahr | | | Zeit | Tag | Monat | Jahr |

their reduced structure. Special report follows. Emissary Kasche has send the

von   waren   an   durch

appropriate message to the Foreign Office in Berlin and asks for directives as to

Telegramm — Funkspruch — Fernschreiben

N.-Ü. whether the establishment can be carried out under the aforementioned

conditions, or whether different procedures should be followed.

BESTIMMEN. ===

Phleps

F.D.R. signed: Renner, SS Obersturmführer

Heftrand

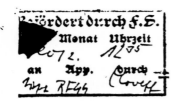

Blitz-Telegraph  **Blitz!**

An das
To the SS Headquarters

7 Ausfertigungen
7.Ausfertigung 20

Berlin

I forward the enclosed message from Reichsführer SS to SS Gruppenführer Phleps and at the same time request that the text be sent to SS Gruppenführer Jüttner.
"To SS Gruppenführer Phleps
Have received report on your talk with Emissary Kasche and Foreign Minister Lorkovic. General Glaise-Horstenau was with me yesterday. The suggestions that Emissary Kasche made there do not correspond with my intentions.

1) I am very happy to accept 6000 Ustascha volunteers for the formation of police battalions and for training as regular policemen. Returned to Croatia after one year.

2) I am sticking to my intention of forming SS Bosniak Division of Moslems, who for the most part are not fighting on our side today, but are standing aside or even fighting against us. As Bosniaks, they would surely be loyal soldiers on our side.

I have notified the Foreign Office personally.

Heil Hitler!

signed: H. Himmler"

Blitz-Telegraph **Blitz!**

XVI/2

Ausfertigungen

Ausfertigung

Dispatch

To the Reich Foreign Minister von Ribbentrop

<u>Berlin</u>

Dear Ribbentrop!

I ask you to take note of the telegram from SS Gruppenführer and Generalleutnant of the Waffen-SS Phleps and my answering telegram:

"To Reichsführer-SS

Report results of my conference in Agram yesterday with Emissary Kasche, Foreign Minister Lorkovic and Oberst Funk, Representative of General Glaise-Horstenau, concerning a Moslem SS division. The Croatian government welcomes its establishment, recruiting by the Germans is not wanted for reasons of internal and foreign policy. Poglavnix places value on the designation of Ustascha Division, Croatian uniforms and insignia of rank, and as much Croatian command language as possible. Formation in the country is desired for reasons of security. Croatia can provide 6000 Ustascha volunteers immediately. In addition, the influencing of the Moslem leader of northeastern Bosnia for recruiting volunteers is affirmed. Great difficulties arise from the formation of officer and junior officer personnel. This Croatian SS Ustascha Division, as they wish it to be designated, cannot be proclaimed as SS. but is rather a Croatian unit established with the help of the SS. Standartenführer Dengel is charged from here with clearing up all questions concerning its formation in advance with the staff of the commanding general in Agram, and then to complete the muster rolls with the help of Croatian officials. The division will be formed, in fact, like the "Prinz Eugen" Division, by omitting special units or forming them in reduced size. A special report on this subject follows; Emissary Kasche has sent a corresponding telegram to the Foreign Office in Berlin and asks for instructions as to whether the establishment shall be carried out under the conditions cited above, or whether further instructions are to determine further procedure.

(signed) Phleps"

"To SS Gruppenführer Phleps
Have received report of your conference with Emissary Kasche and Foreign Minister Lorkovic. General Glaise-Horstenau was with me yesterday. The following suggestions of Emissary Kasche do not represent my views:

1.) I am very happy to accept 6000 Ustascha volunteers to form police battalions and training as regular policemen. Return to Croatia after one year.

2.) I stand by my intention of forming an SS Bosniak division of Moslems, who presently are for the most part not fighting on our side, but rather standing aside or even fighting against us. As Bosniaks, they would surely be loyal soldiers on our side.

I have informed the Foreign Office of my position.

Heil Hitler!

Yours

(signed) H. Himmler"

20.2.1943
Bra/Br.

Fernspruch · Fernschreiben · Funkspruch · Blinkspruch

Nachr.-Stelle	Nr.	Befördert				
		an	Tag	Zeit	durch	Rolle
SS-Führungshauptamt -Schreibstelle-	0579	952				

Vermerke: Geheime Kommandosache

Angenommen oder aufgenommen				**Befördert**		
von	Tag	Zeit	durch	25 Tag 2. Monat 1730 Uhrzeit		
WAGB	25.2.	0500	SFHS	an _____ durch _____		

Abgang	An		Absendende Stelle
Tag: 24.2.	Reichsführer-SS H i m m l e r		WAGB 0479
Zeit: 2005	Führerhauptquartier		25.2.43 0200
Dringlichkeits-Vermerk			Fernsprech-Anschluß:

From German commanding general in Croatia, Unit 1b/Org. 15 No. 0386/43, secret command material, for personal information of the Reichsführer. The conference with Poglavnik, reported by Gruppenführer Phleps yesterday, the 23rd day of the month, had the purpose of determining, in the absence of the emissary on official duty, whether the groundwork for the establishment of a Bosniak division was already fully prepared politically. This was true only in part. The Croatian government greets the idea most warmly in principle, but would prefer to make available on its own 20,000 of its Ustascha volunteers, including Moslems. It requests, not without justification, foreign political cover by us to avoid very probable Italian countermeasures, such as the reorganization of Serbian Cetnici formations into black-shirt divisions or recent permission for Cetnici departures for Croatian settlements. It seems to me that the Croatian domestic considerations, concentrated against our intention of carrying out the recruitment of Croatian volunteers ourselves and concentrating on the Bosnian Moslems, are not necessarily valid, since these Moslems, despite their undoubtedly Croatian blood, see themselves as an

individual ethnic community and can therefore also be utilized as
such militarily, whereby is must be kept in mind that in many cases
they found ways to avoid their military obligations to the Croatian
state. It might rather be noted that in the meantime Vice-Minister-
President Kulenovic, the official leader of the Bosnian Moslems,
expressed his doubts as to the possibility of success of the recruitment of volunteers planned by us among his co-religionists. In
1941, Kulenovic stated, not 20,000, but 100,000 Bosnian Moslems
had volunteered for German service, but now only a modest frac-
tion of that number was to be reckoned with. The use of the term
Ustacha (which means insurgent or rebel) desired by Croatia in the
title of the new division seems impractical to me.

It appears that Poglavnik will strive to set up, via the Reich Foreign Minister, a meeting between you and the Croatian Foreign
Minister Lorkovic. In view of the political side of the question,
considerable at the beginning, Phleps and I have stepped out of the
situation for the time being. I ask you to view this message, in the
spirit of our last discussion, as a purely personal one.

(signed) Glaise

German Commanding General in Croatia

Unit 1b/Org.15 No. 0386/43 Secret Command Material

F.d.k.d.Entschl.

SS Obersturmführer

Telegram

to the
German Commanding General in Croatia
General Glaise

Telegram of 2/25/1943 received with thanks. Your personal observations are very valuable to me. I am making immediate contact with the Reich Foreign Minister for the purpose of carrying out my intention of an SS division purely of Moslem Bosniaks. I hope thereby to make an ethnic group that today is standing aside because of the conditions in the Croatian state and has a great tradition and loyalty to the Reich militarily valuable to us. The use of the title "Ustascha" for this division is definitely not possible. I am looking forward very much to a conference with Foreign Minister Lorkovic. I'll advise you later as soon as I have discussed these matters with the Reich Foreign Minister on his return.

(signed) H. Himmler

3/3/1943

2.) SS Gruppenführer Berger
Copy with request to take note of it.

I.A. (signature)

SS Obersturmbannführer

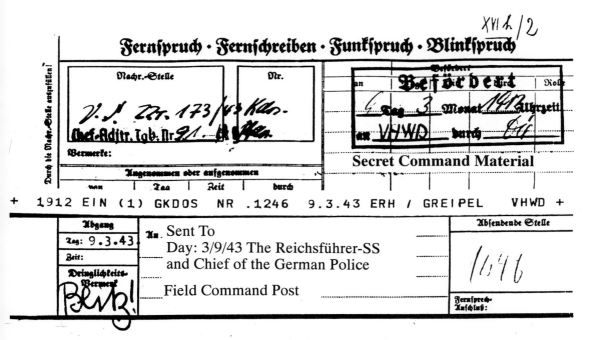

Secret Command Material

+ 1912 EIN (1) GKDOS NR .1246 9.3.43 ERH / GREIPEL VHWD +

Sent To
Day: 3/9/43 The Reichsführer-SS
and Chief of the German Police

Field Command Post

Cd#HA/Be/Vo. VS-Tgb.Nr. 173 /43 g.Kdos.
C.Adj.   VS-Tgb.Nr. 91 /43 g.Kdos.

3 Ausfertigungen
Prüf.Nr.

Reichsführer!

1.)
The negotiations regarding the Bosniak division are completed. Agreement of both sides was achieved. The Croatian government believes, though, that before the agreed-on terms are carried out, the Italian government's agreement must be obtained.

2).
Mustering for the "Prinz Eugen" Division is beginning.

3.)
The suggestion of the SS main office to organize older men taken out of "Prinz Eugen" Division into local defense and village protection units for the use of the Ethnic Group Leader is being sabotaged by Emissary Kasche. He wants to put these men at the disposal of the Croatian Defense Ministry. I ask for support in allowing these men to go home under any conditions, since

	Fernspruch	Nr.	Von	An	Tag	Zeit	Annehmender Offz. (Uffz.)	
	Fernschreiben						Name	Dienstgrad
	Funkspruch							
	Blinkspruch							

SSV K 83a ##-Vordruckverlag 28. F. Mayr Miesbach (Bayer Hochland) 14628

Fernspruch · Fernschreiben · Funkspruch · Blinkspruch

Nachr.-Stelle		Nr.		Befördert				
			an	Tag	Zeit	durch	Rolle
Vermerke:								
Angenommen oder aufgenommen								
von	Tag	Zeit	durch					

Abgang	An	Absendende Stelle
Tag: 9.3.43.	den Reichsführer-SS und	
Zeit:	Chef der Deutschen Polizei,	
Dringlichkeits-Vermerk	Feld-Kommandostelle.	Fernsprech-Anschluß:

— 2 —

a)
it concerns a.v. and g.v.H. men over 40,

b)
the German communities are without any protection, and

c)
the spring planting is endangered.

SS-Gruppenführer

(signature) SS Gruppenführer

		Nr.	Von	An	Tag	Zeit	Annehmender Offz. (Uffz.)	
							Name	Dienstgrad
Quittung	Fernspruch Fernschreiben Funkspruch Blinkspruch							

8V K 83a SS-Vordruckverlag W. J. Mayr Miesbach (Bayer. Hochland) 14522

SS Main Command Office
Command Office, Waffen-SS
Daybook No. 589/43 Secret

Berlin-Wilmersdorf, April 30, 1943
Kaiserallee 188

Secret Command Material

Re: Establishment of the Croatian SS Volunteer Division.
Copies: 1 - (goes only to offices involved).

Sender: Special Sender: 70 Copies

1.) As commanded by the Führer on 2/10/1943, the
        "Croatian SS Volunteer Division" (Kroat.SS-Freiw.Div.)
will be established for the time being according to the enclosed system.

2.) The tactical structure of the Croatian SS Volunteer Division will be directed only by the involved offices and the SS Gruppenführer and Generalleutnant of the Waffen-SS Phleps.

3.) Day of establishment: March 1, 1943

4.) The place of establishment is still to be ordered.

5.) Filling of command positions:

   a) For the time being, ethnic German active and reserve officers from Croatia, as well as Moslem active and reserve officers, are available.

   b) The Division is to strive particularly for the quick development of Moslem successor officers.

   c) The classification of the aforementioned ethnic German, Croatian and Moslem officers will take place so that the allowances are guaranteed according to their rank at that time in the Croatian Army, but their rank will be one rank lower during a six-month probation period, especially for officers with longer service. After this six-month probation period, they will be accepted as officers for the duration of the war. Transfer to the police with their rank in the Croatian Army will take place in case of incomplete physical or military achievement. Those not suitable in physical or personal terms will be discharged.

   d) Officers of the medical or administrative services will be provided by the SS Main Command Office, Group D or the Personnel Office of the SS Main Office. The SS Main Office Court will set up the court of the Croatian SS Volunteer Division.

6.) Filling the ranks of junior officers and men with volunteers from the territory of the independent state of Croatia (only Moslems). If individual positions cannot be filled from these volunteers, only native or ethnic Germans may be transferred to this division.

7.) The establishment of the Division Intelligence Unit in Goslar is already commanded by Instruction SS-FHA, Command Office, Waffen-SS, Daybook No. II/2957/43. of 4/27/43.

8.) Shipment of weapons, equipment and vehicles will be done by special order of the SS Main Command Office, Section Ib.

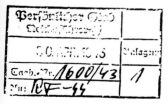

9.) Assignment of <u>motor vehicles</u> will be done by special order of SS-FHA, Office X.

10.) <u>Horses</u> will be supplied on request by SS-FHA, Office VI.

11.) <u>KSt and KAN</u> will be supplied by SS-FHA, Command Office d.W.-SS,Abt.Org./StAN, <u>instructions</u> on request from the division by SS-FHA, Regulation and Instructional Material Office. Special order for equipping with instructions follows.

12.) <u>Field Postal Numbers</u> will be assigned by SS-FHA, Office II, Section Ic/Fp.

13.) The assigning of <u>field postal</u> and <u>field police troops</u> will be done by SS-FHA, Office II, Section Ic.

14.) <u>Clothing and supplies</u> of the division as mountain divisions. The uniform is that of the Waffen-SS with the following modifications:

    a) Emblems for the collar patches remain to be ordered.

    b) A field-gray fez will be worn with the service uniform.

    c) Each man will have a red fez for his parade and dress uniforms.

    d) Officers are allowed to wear the mountain cap with their dress uniform.

    e) SS members will wear the Sigrunes on their left breast. Each man of the division will wear a red and white emblem of the pattern approved by the Reichsführer-SS on his right upper arm.

15.) Payment, supplying and care will be handled as with the other SS volunteer legions assigned to the Waffen-SS as well as the other Croatian legion troops of the German Wehrmacht.

16.) The service and command language is <u>German</u>, the training and everyday language is <u>Croatian</u>.

17.) The Croatian SS Volunteer Division is subordinate during training, and until further orders arrive, to the SS Command Main Office. For the time being,

SS Standartenführer von Obwurzer

is responsible for its establishment.
The division staff is to be set up in Agram.
Address: Field Post Number 57400.
Telephone access via the "German Commanding

                           General in Agram",
                           number Agram 8300.

                           (signed) Jüttner

                           SS Gruppenführer and
                           Generalleutnant of the Waffen-SS

F.d.R.
(signature)

SS Obersturmbannführer.

The Reichsführer-SS   Field Command Post,   July 1943

To the Deputy of the Reichsführer-SS in Croatia
SS Brigadenführer and Generalmajor of Police Kammerhofer

————

I am absolutely dissatisfied with the support of the establishment of the Croatian SS Volunteer Division ordered by the Führer. Along with many other details, which SS Standartenführer Obwurzer will communicate to you, I object above all to the following points.

1.) I have received reports that among Croatian military offices in the regions where volunteers have reported to the SS Volunteer Division, wild recruiting has been done in the night, with young men being hauled out of bed and placed in barracks of the Croatian Army. Since I suspect that these offices belong to concealed Communistic or Cetkini bands, I charge you to intervene immediately with the police in these areas.

2.) I also charge you to examine the inmates of the Croatian concentration camps in Novogradisca and Jasenovac. I have received definite and very clear reports that in these areas as well, young men were not only taken to Croatian barracks, but simply because of the fact that they reported to us, were taken to the concentration camps. It is obvious that these actions could have been carried out only by enemies of the Croatian state. Here too, you are to use all your powers to intervene. I want a complete report from you that the inmates of the two concentration camps have been checked by our organization. Likewise I want a report that the guilty enemies of the Croatian state have been held responsible in the strictest way. It is best to take them to the concentration camps. In many cases the death penalty will be appropriate.

3.) I have not yet received the list of the volunteers as ordered by the ministry of the armed forces on 5/15/1943. I cannot help but suspect that this order of the Croatian state and thus of the Poglavnik has been sabotaged by enemies of the Croatian state.

4.) I expect that in the troop units of the Croatian Army, which consist predominantly of Moslems, we can set up recruitment evenings for the members of the replacement center, to be followed by immediate turning over and marching away of the volunteers who have reported. I must make this demand because my trust in the loyal carrying out of the terms agreed on has disappeared very strongly.

5.) I expect your report on the complete establishment of the division with a strength of about 26,000 men by 8/1/1943. I commission you to inform the German Ambassador, the German General in Agram, as well as the appropriate Croatian national agencies of these orders of mine.

The Reichsführer-SS   Field Command Post, July 3, 1943
Daybook No. 1670145
RF/Bn

Secret Government Materials

3 Copies

2nd Copy

To the Chief of the SS Main Office
SS Obergruppenführer Berger

Berlin

      I instruct that the sum of up to 2,000,000 Reichsmark be made available to the Deputy of the Reichsführer-SS in Croatia for the recruitment of of Croatian SS Volunteer Division and the German Police in Croatia. The transfer of the first half million must take place without delay within the next 24 hours in the usual manner.

SS Command Office
Office II Org.Abt.Ia/II
Berlin-Wilmersdorf
Kaiserallee 188
Daybook No. 1667/44 secret

Secret Command Material

Re: Establishment of the Waffen-SS Mountain Division (Croatian No. 2)
Copies: -3- (only to the Division and the General Command (Mtn.) Waffen-SS A.K.)

Sender   Special Sender   78 Copies
                                                            Copy No. 2

I.) 1.)   The Führer has commanded the formation of the

          Waffen-SS Mountain Division (Croatian No. 2)
                 (Waffen-Geb.Div.-SS (kroat.Nr.2)
          and assigned it the name "Kama."

   2.)   Formation area: Save-Bosna-Spreca-Drina.

   3.)   Formation beginning: June 10, 1944.

II.)1.)   For the establishment of the Waffen-SS Mountain Division "Kama"
          (Croatian No. 2), the Commanding General of the
          General Command Waffen-SS (Mtn.)A.K., SS Brigadenführer and
          Generalmajor of the Waffen-SS Sauberzweig, is responsible.

   2.)   The Division Commander will be appointed by the Reichsführer-SS.

III.)   Structure:

          The Waffen-SS Mountain Division "Kama" (Croatian No. 2) is to be set up
          according to Enclosure 1. The list of validity of KSt and KAN is enclosed
          as Enclosure 2.
          Institution of new KSt and KAN for the list of validity no longer has to be
          done according to the directions in the AHM as of 7/1/1944, or after the
          appearance of the KSt and KAN, but will always be commanded by the
          SS-FHA in the V.Bl.d.W.-SS or by special orders. Changes in the KSt and
          KAN are to be made according to the directions in the AHM.

IV.)   Subordination:

          The Waffen-SS Mountain Division "Kama" (Croatian No. 2) is to be
          subordinate for action and troop service to the General Command
          (Mtn.), Waffen-SS A.K.

V.)1.) Formation:

a) Div. Staff		Formed in Croatian area by Mtn.Cmd. Waffen-(Mtn.)A.K.-SS
b) Div.Map Unit Survey & Ranging Platoon/Art.Reg.	)))	Formed Mtn. SS Art. School, Glau_ By SS FHA In 4
c) Field Police Tr Field Post Office	))	Formed SS Driver & Repl. Unit, Weimar-Buchenwald, By SS FHA, Section 1c.
d) 2 Mtn. Jäger		Formed in Croatian area Regiments By Gen. Cmd. Waffen-(Mtn.)A.K.-SS
e) Intelligence Unit		Formed in Croatian area By Gen. Cmd. Waffen-(Mtn.)A.K.-SS
f) Panzerjäger Unit		Formed in Croatian area By Gen. Cmd. Waffen-(Mtn.)A.K.-SS
g) Artillery Regt. minus survey & ranging unit	)))	Formed in Croatian area By SS FHA, In 4.

13th Waffen-SS Mtn. Div. "Handschar" (Croatian No. 1) provides from SS A.R. 13 one battery per unit personnel.
13th Waffen-SS Mtn. Div. "Handschar" (Croatian No. 1) receives recruits in exchange.

h) Engineer	Formed (personnel) at SS Eng. School, Battalion Hradischko, by SS FHA, In. 5.
i) Intelligence	Formed in Croatian area Unit By Gen. Cmd. Waffen-(Mtn.)A.K.-SS

Essential personnel to be provided by SS Intelligence Unit 13. Recruits will be provided to fill SS Intelligence Unit 13.

k) Field Repl. Btl.	Formed in Croatian area By Gen. Cmd. Waffen-(Mtn.)A.K.-SS
l) Div. Supply Troop	Formed in Croatian area By Gen. Cmd. Waffen-(Mtn.)A.K.-SS
m) Repair Shop Co.	Formed at SS Tank Repair Training & Repl. Unit, Oranienburg By SS FHA, Section X
n) Admin. Trp. Unit	Formed at Training & Repl. Unit of SS Admin. Services, Dachau By SS FHA, Section IV
o) Medical Services	Formed in Croatian area by Gen. Cmd. Waffen-(Mtn.)A.K.-SS
p) Veterinary Co.	Formed in Croatian area By SS FHA, Section VI

(Still V)

2.)   Training:

a) Special instruction for training of officers and junior officers for the Artillery Regiment is to be carried out at the SS Artillery School II in Bebeschau. SS FHA In 4. is responsible for carrying this out.

b) Other specialists are to be assembled and trained after recruitment in collaboration with the Inspection of the SS FHA.

3.)   <u>Formation and training must be completed by 12/31/44 and be reported to the SS FHA Org.Abt.Ia by the stated date.</u>

VI.)   Personnel Procedures

1.)   With assigning of German commanders. Junior officers and men from the SS Main Command Office can be expected only in small numbers.

Commanders of the administrative services will be supplied by the Personnel Office of the SS W.V. Main Office.

2.)   Positions in the Waffen-SS Mtn. Div. "Kama" (Croatian No. 2) must be filled predominantly with Croatian nationals.

VII.)   Material Procedures:

1.   Shipment of weapons, equipment, motor and other vehicles will be done according to Special Order from SS FHA, Section II, Org.Abt.Ib.

Supply of all material equipment with exception of that for Div. Map Unit, Survey & Ranging Platoon/Art.Reg., Field Police Troop, Field Post Office and Repair Shop Co. will be done in the formation area.

If supply of weapons for the Panzerjäger Platoon (3 7.5 cm guns) for the Panzerjäger Companies of the Mountain Jäger Regiments is changed, they will be supplied with medium Pak guns or organized as an antitank platoon.

2.)   Medical material, equipment and supplies will be provided on request to SS FHA, Unit D, Section XV via the ZSL (Central Medical Depot by Reichs Doctor-SS and Police).

3.)   Supplying of KSt and KAN will be done by SS FHA Section II. Org.Abt.Ia/II without request.

4.)   As to supplying of instruction, Special Order of the SS FHA Section Id. applies.

VIII.)   Payment and compensation will be done according to the guidelines provided by the SS W.V. Main Office.

IX.)   Field Post numbers will be provided by SS FHA, Section Ic/ Fp without request.

X.)   For uniform preparation of the condition reports for submission beginning on 4/20/44, act according to order of OKH GenStdH/Org.Abt.I/3600/43 g.Kdos. of 8/1/43 and SS FHA Section II, Org.Abt.__, Daybook No. II/ 5929/44. As of 7/10 /1944, these are to be done exclusively by the new wartime organization with the established specified strengths of personnel and materials as well as horses.

The specified and actual strengths of personnel, materials and horses are to be entered on the specified days according to wartime organization.

XI.)   a)   The actual strength of personnel entered according to wartime organization as per Item X must include all soldiers on hand. This also includes those on leave, detailed elsewhere, sick and wounded within 8 weeks, and any available supernumerary soldiers.

As opposed to the specified strength (number of available soldiers and aides established by KStN), the actual strength differs only by the number of available soldiers above or below the specified strength.

b)   The actual strength of material entered according to Item X includes all material items available on the specified day (specified truck equipment includes the available towing tractors).

(Still XI)

    c)   The total actual strength of horses entered according to Item X is to include all available horses including those sick or detailed away.

    d)   The specified number of trucks is to include all motor vehicles with truck chassis, except passenger vehicles with light truck chassis.

XII.)   <u>New Nomenclature:</u>

According to regulation OKH GenStdH/Org.Abt. Daybook No. 1/15710/ 44 g./Kdos. II.Ang. of 2/25/44, the assault gun batteries within the Panzerjäger units of the Mountain Division are to be renamed "Assault Gun Units" while retaining their KStN and wartime structure subordination.

The leader of each such unit (previously Battery Leader) is to be called "Leader Assault Gun Unit" (not Unit Commander).

The tactical symbol of the Assault Gun Unit of each Panzerjäger Unit it to be determined by wartime structure.

(signed) Jüttner

F.d.R. [signature]

SS Hauptsturmführer.

SS Main Command Office   Berlin-Wilmersdorf, June 24, 1944
Section II Org.Abt.Ia/II   Kaiserallee 188

Teletype Message

For transmission to:
70 Copies

1.) Gen.Comm.V SS(Mtn.)Corps   Copy 2
2.) B.d.W. SS "Hungary"
3.) Gen.Comm. Waffen-SS Mtn. Army Corps
     via 13th Waffen-SS Mtn. Div. "Handschar."

Intelligence:

18th SS Volunteer Panzer-Grenadier Div. "Horst Wessel"
13th Waffen-SS Mtn. Div. "Handschar"
Reichsführer-SS

Re: SS FHA, Section II Org.Abt.Ia/II, Daybook No. 1530/44, secret command
     material, v.6/6/44.
     SS FHA, Section II Org.Abt.Ia/II, Daybook No. 1667/44, secret command
     material, v.6/17/44.

1.) As commanded by the Führer, the formation of the General Command
Waffen-SS (Mtn.) Army Corps and Waffen-SS Mtn.Div. "Kama", as opposed
to previous orders, will take place in the area of the 18th SS Volunteer Panzer-
Grenadier Div. "Horst Wessel" in southern Hungary.

2.) The 18th Volunteer Panzer-Grenadier Div. "Horst Wessel" is therefore to be
transferred at once to the former area of the 16th SS Panzer-Grenadier Div.
"RF-SS" (Debrecin). The B.d.W. SS "Hungary" is responsible for the transfer.

3.) Transfer of the already existing sections of General Command, Waffen-SS (Mtn.)
Army Corps and Waffen-SS Mtn. Div. "Kama" will be led by General Com-
mand Waffen-SS (Mtn.) Army Corps in direct understanding with B.d.W. SS
"Hungary" on their own responsibility.

4.) a) General Command Waffen-SS (Mtn.) Army Corps and Waffen-SS Mtn.
     Div. "Kama" are located unconditionally in the new formation area of the
     SS-FHA.
     In territorial situations they are subordinate to the B.d.W. SS "Hungary."

   b) The 13th Waffen-SS Mtn. Div. "Handschar" remains in the previous area
     and is tactically subordinated to General Command V, SS (Mtn.) Army
     Corps.

(Still 4.) b)

In terms of organization and in its political and economic duties of satisfaction, the Division is subordinate as previously to the General Command, Waffen-SS (Mtn.) Army Corps.

5.) Completed transfers are to be reported via B.d.W. SS "Hungary" or General Command Waffen-SS (Mtn.) Army Corps by teletype to SS FHA Org.Abt.Ia.

SS FHA, Section II Org.Amt.Ia.II
Daybook No. 1919/44,secret command material

signed Jüttner

F.d.R.

Koch

SS Hauptsturmführer

153

SS Main Command Office   Berlin-Wilmersdorf
Section II Org.Abt.Ia/II   Kaiserallee 188
Daybook No. 1666/44 secret

Secret Command Material

Re: Wartime structure of SS Volunteer Div. "Prinz Eugen", 13th Waffen-SS Mtn.
Div. "Handschar" (Croatian No. 1) and Waffen- SS Mtn. Div. "Skanderbeg"
(Albanian No. 1).

                                                        73 Copies
Sender: Special Sender   Test No. 2 Anlg. 3

1.) Relevant wartime structures, lists of validity and relevant KStN are in force as
of 7/10/1944.
7th SS Volunteer Mtn. Div. "Prinz Eugen", 13th Waffen-SS Mtn.Div.
"Handschar" (Croatian No. 1) and Waffen-SS Mtn. Div. "Skanderbeg" (Albanian No. 1) are to be structured thus:

2.) Corresponding to mountain service, the KStN for Mtn. Jäger regiments and
Mtn. Engineer Battalions are included in the validity lists.

In case of transfer of a Mtn. Div. to a flatland front, the changes in the KStN
will be ordered specifically via SS FHA, Org.Abt.Ia/II.

3.) a) Reorganization or new organization of the Panzer-Jäger Units must be carried out by the Division in terms of personnel and material, using available
supplies of personnel and materials.

b) The Assault Gun Battery ordered organized according to orders from SS
FHA, Command Office, Waffen-SS, Org. Daybk. No. II/5046/43, as of
7/8/43, and transferred to General Command, V. SS)Mtn.) Army Corps, is
disbanded and the personnel and materials transferred as Assault Gun Unit
to Panzer-Jäger Unit 7, SS Volunteer Mtn. Div. "Prinz Eugen."

c) The Panzer Company ordered organized according to orders from SS FHA,
Org. Daybook No. 1880/42 as of 4/1/42 and transferred to General Command, V. SS (Mtn.) Army Corps, is disbanded and the personnel and materials transferred as Assault Gun Unit to the Panzer-Jäger Unit of the Waffen-
SS Mtn. Div. "Skanderbeg" (Albanian No. 1).

In the course of instructions via OKH, the tanks will be exchanged for
assault guns or 38 t tank destroyers.

(still 3)

d) According to OKH GenStdH/Org.Abt.Daybook No. I/15710/44, secret II.Ang. instructions of 2/25/44, the Assault Gun Battery in the Panzer-Jäger Units of the Mountain Divisions will be renamed "Assault Gun Unit" while retaining its KStN and wartime structure subordination.

The leader of this unit (formerly Battery Leader) is called "Führer, Assault Gun Unit" (not Unit Commander).

The tactical symbol of the Assault Gun Unit of the Panzer- Jäger Unit of the Mountain Division will be that used in the wartime structure.

e) The 2 cm Companies of SS Flak Unit 7 and SS Flak Unit 13 will be transferred with personnel and material to the Panzer-Jäger Units of the 7th SS Volunteer Mtn. Div. "Prinz Eugen" and the 13th Waffen-SS Mtn. Div. "Handschar" (Croatian No. 1).

4.) a) The SS Flak Unit 7 (without 1 2cm Flak Co.) being removed from the 7th SS Volunteer Mtn. Div. "Prinz Eugen" will, according to special orders from SS FHA, be assigned as a command troop to General Command, V. SS (Mtn.) Army Corps, and subordinated to it.

b) SS Flak Unit 13 (without 1 2cm Flak Co.) will, according to special orders from SS FHA, be assigned as a command troop to the general Command, Waffen-SS (Mtn.) Army Corps, and subordinated to it.

5.) For the uniform preparation of the situation reports to be submitted according to orders from OKH GenStdH/ Org.Abt. I/3600/43, secret material, of 8.1.43, and SS FHA, Section II, Org.Abt. Daybook No. II/5929/44, of 4/20/44, these are, as of 7/10/1944, to be based exclusively on the new wartime structures with the determined specified strengths of personnel and materials, as well as horses.

The applicable specified and actual strengths of personnel on the day in question, the specified and actual amounts of equipment, and the specified and actual numbers of horses, are to be recorded in the wartime structure reports.

6.) a) The actual personnel strength to be entered under No. 5 on the wartime structure report must include all soldiers on the muster rolls. This includes men on leave, detailed away, sick and wounded within 8 weeks, and any present supernumerary soldiers.

As opposed to the specified (number of applicable soldiers and helpers according to KStN), the actual strength can differ only by the number of missing men or available men above the specified number.

b) The actual material strength to be entered under No. 5 includes all materials available on the day in question (specified truck equipment includes the available towing tractors).

c) The actual strength of horses to be entered under No. 5 must include all available horses including those sick or detailed away.

d) The actual number of trucks must include all motor vehicles with truck chassis, except passenger vehicles with light truck chassis.

7.) The institution of new KSt and KAN for the validity lists as of 7/1/1944 is no longer to ne done according to the specifications in the AHM or the KSt and KAN, but will rather be ordered by the SS FHA in V.Bl.d.W.-SS or by special orders. From now on, changes in the KSt and KAN are to be made according to the specifications in the AHM.

8.) For the first time, the situation report of 7/15/44 is to report the condition of restructuring to the Reichsführer- SS and SS Main Command Office.

9.) Weapons and equipment missing on account of restructuring are to be requested from SS FHA, Org.Abt.Ib.

Equipping of the Panzer-Jäger Platoon (3 7.5 cm guns) of the Mountain Jäger Regiments with heavy Pak guns as far as still available, otherwise equipping with medium Pak guns or organization as Tank Destroyer Platoons.

10.) <u>Renaming:</u>

The food supply office will be renamed

Administrative Company.

signed Jüttner

.d.R. (signature)

SS Hauptsturmführer.

X. Footnotes

1. Kaltenegger, Roland, Die deutsche Gebirgstruppe 1935-1945, Munich 1989, pp. 39ff.
2. Kaltenegger, Roland, Kampf der Gebirgsjäger um die Westalpen und den Semmering. Die Kriegschroniken der 8. und 9. Gebirgs-Division (Kampfgruppe Semmering). Graz, Stuttgart 1987, pp. 135ff.
3. Ibid., pp. 173 ff.
4. Compare K. W. Böhme, Die deutschen Kriegsgefangenen in Jugoslawien 1941-1953, Vol. I/1-I/2, Munich 1962-1964. (= Zur Geschichte der deutschen Kriegsgefangenen des Zweiten Weltkrieges.)
5. Kaltenegger, Roland, Schicksalsweg und Kampf der "Bergschuh"-Division, vormals 99. leichte Infanterie-Division, Graz, Stuttgart 1985, pp. 167ff.
6. Keltenegger, Roland, Die Geschichte der deutschen Gebirgstruppe 1915 bis heute. Vom deutschen Alpenkorps des Ersten Weltkrieges zur 1. Gebirgsdivision der Bundeswehr. Stuttgart 1980, pp. 116ff.
7. Ibid, pp. 119ff. See also Roger James Bender and Hugh Page Taylor, Uniforms, organization and history of the Waffen-SS, Vol. 1-3, California 1971-72.
8. Tessin, Georg, Verbände und Truppen der deutschen Wehrmacht und Waffen-SS in Zweiten Weltkrieg 1939-1945, Frankfurt/Main, Osnabrück 1966-1977. Vol. 14, pp. 183ff.
9. Later SS Division "Wallonie" with Commander Leon Degrelle, the best-known and most decorated officer of foreign volunteers in the Waffen-SS.
10. Tessin, Georg, Verbände und Truppen der deutschen Wehrmacht und Waffen-SS, Vol. 3, pp. 44ff.
11. Kaltenegger, Roland, Generaloberst Dietl. Der Held von Narvik. Eine Biographie. Munich 1990, pp. 322ff.
12. Kaltenegger, Roland, Schicksalsweg und Kampf der "Bergschuh"-Division, pp. 183ff.
13. Ibid., pp. 229ff.
14. Schreiber, Franz, Kampf unter dem Nordlicht. Deutsch-finnische Waffenbrüderschaft am Polarkreis. Die Geschichte der 6. SS-Gebirgs-Division Nord. Osnabrück 1969.
15. Tessin, Georg, Verbände und Truppen der deutschen Wehrmacht und Waffen-SS, Vol. 3, p. 83.
16. Kriegstagebuch des Oberkommandos der Wehrmacht (Wehrmacht Command Staff) 1940-1945, compiled by Helmuth Greiner and Percy Ernst Schramm. Ed. by Percy Ernst Schramm for the Arbeitskreis für Wehrforschung. Frankfurt/Main 1963-1969, Vol. III/2, p. 1344.
17. Ibid., p. 1372.
18. Schmitz, Peter, and Klaus-Jürgen Theis, Die Truppenkennzeichen der Verbände und Einheiten der deutschen Wehrmacht und Waffen-SS und ihre Einsätze im Zweiten Weltkrieg 1939-1945. Osnabrück 1987, Vol. 2, pp. 407ff.
19. Kriegstagebuch des Oberkommandos der Wehrmacht, Vol. IV/2, p. 1213.
20. Kumm, Otto, Vorwärts "Prinz Eugen." Kriegsgeschichte der 7. SS Geb.Div. Osnabrück, no year.
21. Tessin, Georg, Verbände und Truppen der deutschen Wehrmacht und Waffen-SS, Vol. 3, pp. 282ff.
22. Kriegstagebuch des Oberkommandos der Wehrmacht, Vol. IV/1, p. 623.
23. Tessin, Georg, Verbände und Truppen der deutschen Wehrmacht und Waffen-SS, Vol. 3, p. 283.
24. Stein, George H., Geschichte der Waffen-SS, Düsseldorf 1978, p. 165.
25. Schmitz, Peter, and Klaus-Jürgen Theis, Die Truppenkennzeichen der Verbände und Einheiten der deutschen Wehrmacht und Waffen-SS, Vol. 2, p. 426.
26. Stein, George H., Geschichte der Waffen-SS, pp. 165ff.
27. Tessin, Georg, Verbände und Truppen der deutschen Wehrmacht und Waffen-SS, Vol. 4, p. 173.
28. Schmitz, Peter, and Klaus-Jürgen Theis, Die Truppenkennzeichen der Verbände und Einheiten der deutschen Wehrmacht und Waffen-SS, Vol. 2, p. 442.
29. Tessin, Georg, Verbände und Truppen der deutschen Wehrmacht und Waffen-SS, Vol. 4, p. 205.
30. Ibid., Vol. 4, p. 220.
31. Michaelis, Rolf, Chronik der 24. Waffen-Gebirgs (Karstjäger)-Division der SS, Erlangen 1992. See also Roland Kaltenegger, Operationszone "Adriatisches Küstenland." Der Kampf um Triest, Istrien und Fiume 1944-1945. Graz, Stuttgart 1993.
32. Tessin, Georg, Verbände und Truppen der deutschen Wehrmacht und Waffen SS, Vol. 3, p. 46.
33. Ibid., Vol. 3, p. 46.
34. Ibid., Vol. 3, p. 84.
35. Ibid., Vol. 3, p. 84.
36. Kaltenegger, Roland, Kampf der Gebirgsjäger um die Westalpen und den Semmering, pp. 141ff.